Focus on WRITING 3

Colin Ward

John Beaumont, Series Editor
Borough of Manhattan Community College
City University of New York

ALWAYS LEARNING

PEARSON

I dedicate this book to my loving wife, Stefanie—CW

Focus on Writing 3

Pearson Education, 10 Bank Street, White Plains, NY 10606

Staff Credits: The people who made up the ***Focus on Writing 3*** team, representing editorial, production, design, and manufacturing, are Pietro Alongi, Rhea Banker, Danielle Belfiore, Elizabeth Carlson, Nan Clarke, Aerin Csigay, Dave Dickey, Christine Edmonds, Oliva Fernandez, Barry Katzen, Penny Laporte, Jaime Lieber, Tara Maceyak, Amy McCormick, Barbara Perez, Joan Poole, Debbie Sistino, Jane Townsend, Paula Van Ells, and Adina Zoltan.

The Grammar Presentation charts in *Focus on Writing 3* are adapted from *Focus on Grammar 3, Fourth Edition*, by Marjorie Fuchs, Margaret Bonner, and Miriam Westheimer, Pearson Education, White Plains, New York, © 2012.

Cover image: Shutterstock.com
Text composition: ElectraGraphics, Inc.
Text font: New Aster

Library of Congress Cataloging-in-Publication Data
Haugnes, Natasha, 1965–
 Focus on writing. 1 / Natasha Haugnes.
  p. cm.
 Includes index.
 ISBN 0-13-231350-2 — ISBN 0-13-231352-9 — ISBN 0-13-231353-7 — ISBN 0-13-231354-5 —
 ISBN 0-13-231355-3 1. English language—Textbooks for foreign speakers. 2. English language—
 Rhetoric—Problems, exercises, etc. 3. Report writing—Problems, exercises, etc. I. Title.
 PE1128.H3934 2011
 428.2—dc22

                                                                                    2011014764

PEARSON LONGMAN ON THE **WEB**

Pearsonlongman.com offers online resources for teachers and students. Access our Companion Websites, our online catalog, and our local offices around the world.

Visit us at **pearsonlongman.com**.

Printed in the United States of America
ISBN 10: 0-13-231353-7
ISBN 13: 978-0-13-231353-7

2 3 4 5 6 7 8 9 10—V042—16 15 14 13 12

Contents

To the Teacher

Focus on Writing is a five-level series that prepares students for academic coursework. Each book in the series gives students an essential set of tools to ensure that they master not only the writing process, but also the grammatical structures, lexical knowledge, and rhetorical modes required for academic writing. The series provides an incremental course of instruction that progresses from basic sentences (Book 1) and paragraphs (Books 1–3) to essays (Books 3–5). Grammar presentation and focused grammar practice are correlated to *Focus on Grammar*.

A Process Approach to Writing

Over the past 30 years, the *writing process* approach has become the primary paradigm for teaching writing. As cognitive research shows, writing is a recursive process. When students practice the entire writing process repeatedly with careful guidance, they internalize the essential steps, thereby improving their writing and their confidence in themselves as writers.

Each unit in each book of *Focus on Writing* provides direct instruction, clear examples, and continual practice in the writing process. Students draw on their prior knowledge, set goals, gather information, organize ideas and evidence, and monitor their own writing process. Students write topic-related sentences and use them in a basic paragraph (Book 1); they focus on writing an *introduction*, *body*, and *conclusion* for a paragraph (Books 2–3) or essay (Books 3–5). Whether students are writing a group of related sentences, a paragraph, or an essay, they produce a complete, cohesive piece of writing in *every* unit.

Predictable Step-by-Step Units

Focus on Writing is easy to use. Its predictable and consistent unit format guides students step by step through the writing process.

■ PLANNING FOR WRITING

Students are introduced to the unit theme through an engaging image and high-interest reading. Brainstorming tasks develop critical thinking and serve as a springboard for the unit's writing assignment. Vocabulary building activities and writing tips related to the topic and organizational focus of the unit provide opportunities for students to expand their own writing.

■ STEP 1: PREWRITING

In Book 1, students learn the basics of sentence structure and are encouraged to combine sentences into cohesive paragraphs. They choose between two authentic academic writing assignments, explore their ideas through discussions with classmates, and complete a graphic organizer.

In Books 2–5, students learn the basics of a rhetorical structure (e.g., narration, description, opinion, persuasion, compare-contrast, cause-effect, or problem-solution) and choose between two authentic academic writing assignments. Students explore their ideas through freewriting, share them with classmates, and complete a graphic organizer.

STEP 2: WRITING THE FIRST DRAFT

Explanations, examples, and focused practice help students to prepare for their own writing assignment. Writing tasks guide students through the steps of the writing process as they analyze and develop topic sentences, body sentences, and concluding sentences (Books 1–3) and continue on to draft thesis statements and complete introductions, body paragraphs, and conclusions (Books 3–5). At all levels, students learn how to use transitions and other connecting words to knit the parts of their writing together.

STEP 3: REVISING

Before students revise their drafts, they read and analyze a writing model, complete vocabulary exercises, and review writing tips that they then apply to their own writing. A Revision Checklist tailored to the specific assignment guides students through the revision process.

STEP 4: EDITING

Grammar presentation and practice help students make the connection between grammar and writing. An Editing Checklist ensures students check and proofread their final drafts before giving them to their instructors.

Helpful Writing Tools

Each book in the series provides students with an array of writing tools to help them gain confidence in their writing skills.

- *Tip for Writers* presents a level-specific writing skill to help students with their assignment. The tips include asking *wh-* questions, using conjunctions to connect ideas, identifying audience, using descriptive details, and using pronoun referents.

- *Building Word Knowledge* sections give students explicit instruction in key vocabulary topics, for example, word families, collocations, compound nouns, and phrasal verbs.

- *Graphic organizers* help students generate and organize information for their writing assignment. For example, in Book 1, they fill out a timeline for a narrative paragraph and in Book 3, they complete a Venn diagram for a compare-contrast essay. In the final unit of Books 4 and 5, they use multiple organizers.

- *Sample paragraphs and essays* throughout the units, tied to the unit theme and writing assignments, provide clear models for students as they learn how to compose a topic sentence, thesis statement, introduction, body, and conclusion.

Carefully Targeted Grammar Instruction

Each unit in *Focus on Writing* helps students make the essential link between grammar and writing. The grammar topics for each unit are carefully chosen and correlated to *Focus on Grammar* to help students fulfill the writing goals of the unit.

Online Teacher's Manuals

The online Teacher's Manuals include model lesson plans, specific unit overviews, timed writing assignments, authentic student models for each assignment, rubrics targeted specifically for the writing assignment, and answer keys.

To the Student

Welcome to *Focus on Writing*! This book will help you develop your writing skills. You will learn about and practice the steps in the writing process.

All of the units are easy to follow. They include many examples, models, and of course, lots of writing activities.

Read the explanations on the next few pages before you begin Unit 1.

> Before you begin to write, you need to know what you will write about. To help you, you will see the **writing focus** under the title of the unit. A picture, a short reading, and a **brainstorming** activity will help you get ideas about a topic. Putting your ideas into a **graphic organizer** will help you structure your ideas.

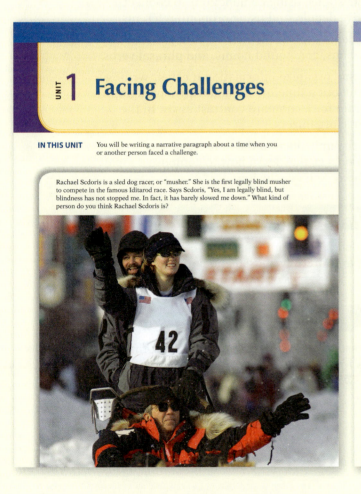

UNIT 1 **Facing Challenges**

IN THIS UNIT You will be writing a narrative paragraph about a time when you or another person faced a challenge.

Rachael Scdoris is a sled dog racer, or "musher." She is the first legally blind musher to compete in the famous Iditarod race. Says Scdoris, "Yes, I am legally blind, but blindness has not stopped me. In fact, it has barely slowed me down." What kind of person do you think Rachael Scdoris is?

Planning for Writing

■ **BRAINSTORM**

A. *Think about the life of Rachael Scdoris. What special challenges do you think she faces when she races? How do you think she handles these challenges? List your ideas below. Share your answers with a partner.*

B. **Using a *Wh-* Questions Chart.** When you are writing about someone's life story, you can ask *who, what, when, where, why,* and *how* questions to gather information. Then you can record the answers on a chart.

Work with a partner. Imagine you are a news reporter writing a story about Rachael Scdoris. What do you want to know about her? What questions will you ask her? Write questions using the wh-words on the chart below.

Who? *Who taught you how to race sled dogs?*
What?
When?
Where?
Why?
How?

3

A **reading** about the topic will help you develop more ideas. The reading can be a newspaper or magazine article, a webpage, or a blog.

Building Word Knowledge activities introduce a vocabulary or dictionary skill that you will be able to use when you write your assignment. For example, you will practice using different word forms and collocations.

A useful **Tip for Writers** gives you specific writing tools, for example, how to use descriptive details and when to use conjunctions to connect ideas.

■ READ

Read the newspaper article about Rachael Scdoris.

Trust in the Snow

Iditarod race route

1   You need a lot of courage to race across 1,500 miles (2,414 km) of snow and ice. You need skill to guide 16 sled dogs through the frozen rivers, forests, and mountains of Alaska. You need endurance[1] to make the 12-day trip from Anchorage to Nome. You need all of this, but you do not need to see.

2   Rachael Scdoris is the first legally blind sled dog racer, or musher, to compete in the Iditarod. In 2005, she made history when she crossed the finish line, taking 57th place out of 72 racers.

3   Since then, she has competed in the race three more times. She reached her dream, but not without facing a number of challenges.

4   Scdoris's dream began at a young age. She has been on a sled since she was three years old and has raced since she was 11. Her father, who raises sled dogs, has been her teacher and support. In 2005, at 19 years old, she was finally prepared to take on the Iditarod.

5   It would not be that easy, however. Scdoris has a rare disorder[2] that limits her vision. She cannot see details or colors. When Scdoris first applied for the Iditarod, she felt frustrated because the racing committee said no.

6   Says Scdoris, "My answer to people who question my ability is: 'Watch me.' I love my dogs, and I am competent[3] in every [part] of the sport, except that every now and then I need a little help seeing things out on the trail."

7   Eventually, Scdoris and her father persuaded the committee to let her race. They allowed Scdoris to have a visual guide. The guide rode behind her and told her by two-way radio if any danger was ahead.

8   The race was, in fact, one of the toughest in Iditarod history. Temperatures dropped to -52 degrees Fahrenheit (-47 degrees Centigrade) and winds blew over 60 miles (97 km) per hour. But Scdoris was determined[4] to meet the challenge. After 12 days, 10 hours, and 42 minutes, she led her dogs across the finish line.

9   Scdoris feels most comfortable and relaxed when racing. "My passion, the reason I believe I exist, is to raise, train, and race sled dogs," she says. "I am a musher, a sled dog racer, and I live for those moments when everything in the universe seems to align[5] into a delicate balance of perfection. In those moments my vision is never an issue."

10   Today, Scdoris has become an inspiration[6] for children and athletes alike, especially those who are disabled.[7] She is not embarrassed about her condition. She gives speeches around the world and repeats the same message: "If you have a passion for it, don't let people tell you you can't."

11   Many people told Scdoris she couldn't, but she has refused to give up. "Yes, I am legally blind," she says, "but blindness has not stopped me. In fact, it has barely slowed me down."

---

[1] **endurance:** the ability to remain strong and patient even though you feel pain or have problems
[2] **disorder:** a disease or illness that prevents part of the body from working correctly
[3] **competent:** having enough skill or knowledge to do something to a satisfactory standard
[4] **determined:** having a strong desire to continue to do something even when it is difficult
[5] **align:** to come together in an organized way and work well together
[6] **inspiration:** someone or something that encourages people to do or produce something good
[7] **disabled:** unable to use a part of the body properly

Building Word Knowledge

Using Participial Adjectives. When writers tell about an event in their own or someone else's life, they often describe people's feelings. In English, writers can use participial adjectives to reveal how someone is feeling. Participial adjectives can be formed by adding *-ed* to regular verbs. "Trust in the Snow" contains examples of participial adjectives that show how Rachael Scdoris felt.

Examples:

In 2005, at 19 years old, she was finally prepared to take on the Iditarod.

When Scdoris first applied for the Iditarod, she felt frustrated.

Reread the article on page 4 and find three more examples of participial adjectives that show how Scdoris was feeling. Circle the sentences and underline the participial adjectives.

Focused Practice

A. Read the Tip for Writers. Then look back at your interview questions from Exercise B on page 3. Did the article answer your questions? Check (✓) "yes" or "no." If you check "yes," write Rachael's answer. The first one is done for you.

> **Tip for Writers**
>
> When you narrate a story, have questions in mind that you want to answer. Asking *wh-* questions (*who, what, when, where, why,* and *how*) will help you gather and include concrete information about the story you want to tell.

	Answered?	Rachael's Answer
Who?	☑ yes ☐ no	*My father taught me to race sled dogs.*
What?	☐ yes ☐ no	
When?	☐ yes ☐ no	
Where?	☐ yes ☐ no	
Why?	☐ yes ☐ no	
How?	☐ yes ☐ no	

B. Read the article again. Mark the statements T (true) or F (false).

_____ 1. The Iditarod takes place in Alaska.

_____ 2. Rachael Scdoris was the first blind musher to compete in the Iditarod.

_____ 3. Scdoris began racing at age three.

_____ 4. Scdoris's mother taught her how to race sled dogs.

_____ 5. Scdoris rode with another musher on her sled.

_____ 6. It took Scdoris about 12 days to complete the Iditarod.

_____ 7. Scdoris believes her blindness hurts her ability to race.

_____ 8. Scdoris speaks to others about her disability.

■ STEP 1: PREWRITING

This section helps you further develop your ideas. It gives you a short explanation of the writing assignment. A small outline gives you a "picture" of the parts of the writing process.

The **Your Own Writing** section gives you a choice of two writing assignments. After you choose one of the assignments, you can begin to think about what you will write and share your ideas with a partner (**Checking in**). Finally, you will complete a **graphic organizer** with ideas for your own writing assignment.

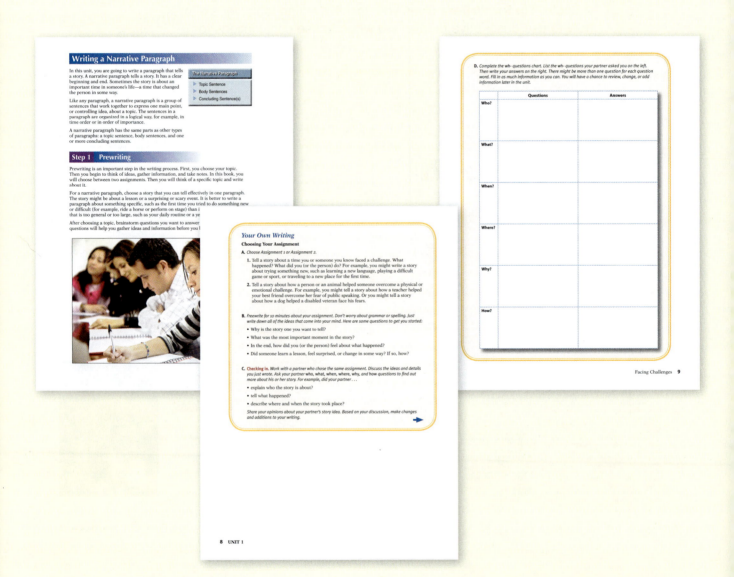

STEP 2: WRITING THE FIRST DRAFT

This section guides you through each part of your writing assignment. For a paragraph assignment, you will learn how to write a topic sentence, body sentences, and concluding sentence(s). For an essay assignment, you will learn how to write a thesis statement, introductory paragraph, body paragraph, and conclusion. At the end of Step 2, you will be able to write a complete first draft.

> **Focused Practice** activities will give you lots of writing practice *before* you draft your writing assignment. Make sure to look at all of the examples and models before you complete the exercises. The outline of the parts of the writing assignment helps you to keep track of where you are in the process.

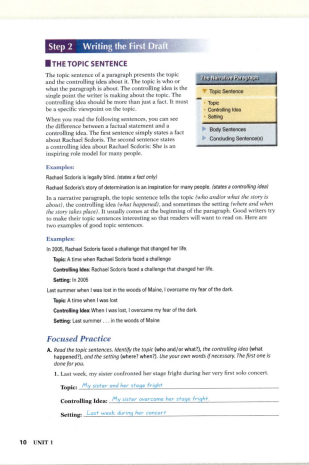

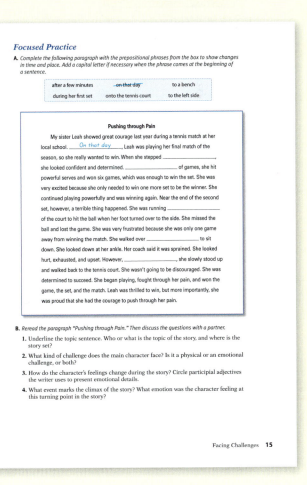

■ STEP 3: REVISING

After you write your first draft, you aren't finished yet! Step 3 shows you how important it is to look again at your writing.

> Review and analyze the **model** paragraphs or essays to get an idea of what a well-written paragraph or essay looks like. You will see how the parts of your own writing should fit together.
>
> Completing the **Revision Checklists** for each writing assignment will help you identify parts of your draft that need improvement.

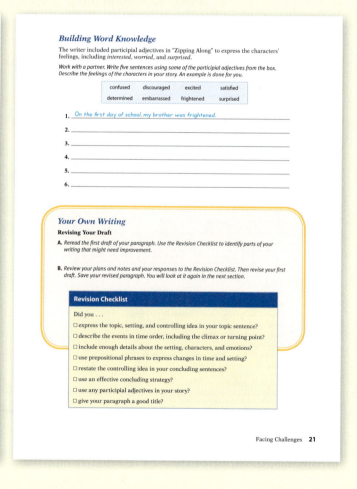

Step 3   Revising

Revising your work is an essential part of the writing process. This is your opportunity to be sure that your paragraph has all the important pieces and that it is clear.

Focused Practice

A. Read the narrative paragraph.

Zipping Along

Two years ago, I faced a big challenge on a trip to Monteverde, Costa Rica, with my friends. My friends asked me to go zip-lining, where people fly through the jungle on a long wire. I was interested, but it also made me nervous. When I woke up in the morning, I felt a little worried. When we got to the site, there was dense fog in the air. The jungle looked mysterious. We walked across a long bridge through the mist, and it felt as if we were floating in air. Then I saw the zip line, and I got scared. It was long, and it disappeared far away into the jungle. When it was my turn, a man hooked me up to the line, and I stepped onto the edge of the platform. My heart was racing and my hands were sweating. I was so high above the forest floor. I told myself to calm down. I took a deep breath and stepped off. I began to fall, and the wind was blowing on my face. I was terrified. I screamed as I went faster and faster through the jungle. Then an amazing thing happened. I opened my eyes, and I felt as free as a bird. I was surprised that I was actually doing it. I was flying! When I got to the other side, I did not want it to end. On that day, I learned that when I face a challenge, I just need to take a deep breath and enjoy the moment.

B. Work with a partner. Answer the questions about the paragraph.

1. What is the controlling idea of the paragraph? Underline the words that state it.
2. What is the setting? Circle the words in the topic sentence that tell you.
3. What words does the writer use to present emotional details about the main character? Check (✔) participial adjectives that explain how the character feels.
4. What event marks the climax or turning point of the story? Put a star at the beginning of the sentence that describes this event.
5. What strategy does the writer use to wrap up or close the story? _____

C. Checking in. Discuss your marked-up paragraph with another pair of students. Then in your group, share one thing about the paragraph that you found the most interesting.

Building Word Knowledge

The writer included participial adjectives in "Zipping Along" to express the characters' feelings, including *interested, worried,* and *surprised.*

Work with a partner. Write five sentences using some of the participial adjectives from the box. Describe the feelings of the characters in your story. An example is done for you.

confused	discouraged	excited	satisfied
determined	embarrassed	frightened	surprised

1. *On the first day of school, my brother was frightened.*
2. _____
3. _____
4. _____
5. _____
6. _____

Your Own Writing

Revising Your Draft

A. Reread the first draft of your paragraph. Use the Revision Checklist to identify parts of your writing that might need improvement.

B. Review your plans and notes and your responses to the Revision Checklist. Then revise your first draft. Save your revised paragraph. You will look at it again in the next section.

> **Revision Checklist**
>
> Did you . . .
> - ☐ express the topic, setting, and controlling idea in your topic sentence?
> - ☐ describe the events in time order, including the climax or turning point?
> - ☐ include enough details about the setting, characters, and emotions?
> - ☐ use prepositional phrases to express changes in time and setting?
> - ☐ restate the controlling idea in your concluding sentences?
> - ☐ use an effective concluding strategy?
> - ☐ use any participial adjectives in your story?
> - ☐ give your paragraph a good title?

■ STEP 4: EDITING

In the final step, you review a grammar topic that will help you edit your revised draft. Then you use an Editing Checklist to correct your own paragraph or essay for any errors in grammar, punctuation, or spelling.

> **Grammar Presentation** charts present notes and examples on specific grammar topics related to your writing assignment. Then you follow up with grammar practice.
>
> **Editing Checklists** for each writing assignment help you correct and polish your final draft.

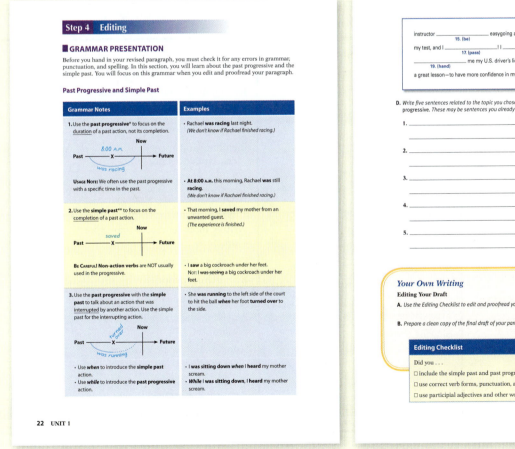

Now, you are ready to begin with Unit 1. Enjoy the writing process!

Scope and Sequence

UNIT	STEP 1 Planning and Prewriting	STEP 2 Writing the First Draft
1 Facing Challenges ***Writing Focus*** Writing a narrative paragraph ***Reading*** *Trust in the Snow*, about Iditarod musher Rachael Scdoris	Using a *wh-* questions chart Using participial adjectives to describe emotions Asking *wh-* questions to gather information Choosing a writing assignment for a narrative paragraph Freewriting about a story Sharing ideas and asking *wh-* questions	Identifying the topic, controlling idea, and setting Writing the topic sentence Using time and place transition words Including emotional details Researching details about a story and taking notes Putting events and details in time order Using a concluding strategy
2 Branded for Success ***Writing Focus*** Writing a descriptive paragraph ***Reading*** *Muzak for the Masses*, about the company Muzak	Using a descriptive web Using word forms correctly Using the conjuction *when* to connect ideas Choosing a writing assignment for a descriptive paragraph Freewriting about the topic Sharing descriptive details	Writing descriptive topic sentences Selecting concrete descriptive words Researching a business, product, or logo Taking notes and citing sources Providing background information Including and arranging descriptive details Using spatial transition words Using a concluding strategy
3 Food for Thought ***Writing Focus*** Writing an opinion paragraph ***Reading*** *All About Corn*, the many uses of this product	Using an opinion chart Using compound nouns Identifying the audience Choosing a writing assignment for an opinion paragraph Freewriting about opinions on a food Sharing opinions	Writing topic sentences that express opinions Using opinion markers Researching a food Taking notes and citing sources Providing and arranging reasons and examples Using *so* and *because* to show cause-effect relationships Summarizing reasons and using a concluding strategy Using a comma with *because*

STEP 3 Revising	STEP 4 Editing	Learning Outcome	*Focus on Grammar Level 3, Fourth Edition*
Analyzing a model narrative paragraph Writing sentences with participial adjectives Applying the Revision Checklist and writing the second draft	Reviewing the past progressive and simple past Incorporating the grammar in sentences and paragraphs Editing a paragraph for grammatical correctness Applying the Editing Checklist and writing the final draft	Can write a description of an event and narrate a story.	**Unit 2** Simple Past **Unit 3** Past Progressive and Simple Past
Analyzing a model descriptive paragraph Writing sentences with different forms of a word Applying the Revision Checklist and writing the second draft	Reviewing indefinite and definite articles Incorporating the grammar in sentences and paragraphs Applying the Editing Checklist and writing the final draft	Can write detailed descriptions on a range of subjects within a field of interest. Can put a series of events into a logical sequence.	**Unit 18** Articles: Indefinite and Definite
Analyzing a model opinion paragraph Forming compound nouns and using them in sentences Applying the Revision Checklist and writing the second draft	Reviewing the modals *can* and *should* Incorporating the grammar in sentences and paragraphs Applying the Editing Checklist and writing the final draft	Can write clear detailed texts on a variety of subjects related to a field of interest. Can synthesize and evaluate information and arguments from a number of sources.	**Unit 13** Ability: *Can, Could, Be able to* **Unit 16** Advice: *Should, Ought to, Had better*

UNIT	STEP 1 Planning and Prewriting	STEP 2 Writing the First Draft
4 Public Spaces *Writing Focus* Writing a persuasive essay *Reading* *A Walk through Past and Present Amman*, about one traveler's view of Amman, Jordan	Using a T-chart Using similes Using descriptive details that appeal to the senses Understanding essays versus paragraphs Choosing a writing assignment for a persuasive essay Freewriting about a point of view on a place Sharing points of view	Writing thesis statements that express an argument or reasoning Providing background information Using opinion markers Researching a place Taking notes and citing sources Linking topic sentences to the thesis statement Including supporting evidence and a summary sentence Restating the thesis and presenting the counterargument and refutation
5 Jobs of the Future *Writing Focus* Writing a compare-contrast essay *Reading* *Jobs: What the Future Holds*, about past and future jobs	Using a Venn diagram Using collocations Determining purpose Understanding comparisons and contrasts Choosing a writing assignment for a compare-contrast essay Freewriting about two jobs Sharing opinions about comparisons	Writing thesis statements that state two topics and key points of comparison Providing background information Using compare-contrast transition words Researching two jobs Taking notes and citing sources Understanding block versus point-by-point methods Using the point-by-point method Restating the thesis and using a concluding strategy
6 Staying Healthy *Writing Focus* Writing a problem-solution essay *Reading* *The Hygiene Hypothesis*, about a theory on effects of excessive cleanliness	Using a problem-solution chart Using phrasal verbs Using pronouns Choosing a writing assignment for a problem-solution essay Researching a topic Freewriting about a health problem, bad habit, or environmental hazard Sharing opinions about problems and solutions	Writing thesis statements that explain a problem and hint at solutions Providing background information Writing topic sentences that transition from problems to solutions Using cause-effect transition words Researching a health problem Taking notes and citing sources Presenting the problem and the solution Including supporting details and summary sentences Restating the thesis and using a concluding strategy

STEP 3 Revising	STEP 4 Editing	Learning Outcome	*Focus on Grammar Level 3, Fourth Edition*
Analyzing a model persuasive essay Analyzing and writing sentences with similes Applying the Revision Checklist and writing the second draft	Reviewing the present perfect: indefinite past Incorporating the grammar in sentences Editing a paragraph for grammatical correctness Applying the Editing Checklist and writing the final draft	Can write an essay that develops an argument, giving reasons in support of or against a particular point of view and explaining the advantages and disadvantages of various options. Can synthesize information and arguments from a number of sources.	**Unit 10** Present Perfect: Indefinite Past
Analyzing a model compare-contrast essay Forming collocations Applying the Revision Checklist and writing the second draft	Reviewing comparisons with *As . . . as* and *Than* Incorporating the grammar in sentences Editing a paragraph for grammatical correctness Applying the Editing Checklist and writing the final draft	Can write an essay that develops an argument systematically with appropriate highlighting of significant points and relevant supporting detail.	**Unit 20** Adjectives: Comparisons with *As . . . as* and *Than*
Analyzing a model problem-solution essay Understanding the meanings of phrasal verbs Applying the Revision Checklist and writing the second draft	Reviewing gerunds: subject and object Incorporating the grammar in sentences and paragraphs Editing a paragraph for grammatical correctness Applying the Editing Checklist and writing the final draft	Can evaluate different ideas or solutions to a problem. Can convey information and ideas on abstract as well as concrete topics, check information and explain problems with reasonable precision.	**Unit 23** Gerunds: Subject and Object

Facing Challenges

IN THIS UNIT   You will be writing a narrative paragraph about a time when you or another person faced a challenge.

Rachael Scdoris is a sled dog racer, or "musher." She is the first legally blind musher to compete in the famous Iditarod race. Says Scdoris, "Yes, I am legally blind, but blindness has not stopped me. In fact, it has barely slowed me down." What kind of person do you think Rachael Scdoris is?

Planning for Writing

■ BRAINSTORM

A. *Think about the life of Rachael Scdoris. What special challenges do you think she faces when she races? How do you think she handles these challenges? List your ideas below. Share your answers with a partner.*

_____

_____

_____

B. Using a *Wh-* Questions Chart. When you are writing about someone's life story, you can ask **who, what, when, where, why,** and **how** questions to gather information. Then you can record the answers on a chart.

Work with a partner. Imagine you are a news reporter writing a story about Rachael Scdoris. What do you want to know about her? What questions will you ask her? Write questions using the wh- words on the chart below.

Who? *Who taught you how to race sled dogs?*
What?
When?
Where?
Why?
How?

3

Read the newspaper article about Rachael Scdoris.

Trust in the Snow

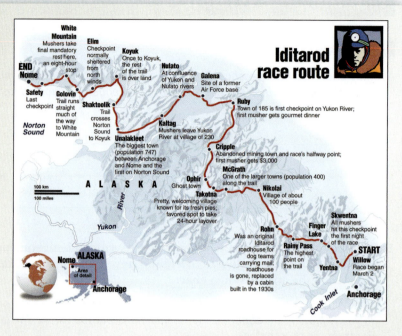

Iditarod race route

White Mountain Mushers take final mandatory rest here, an eight-hour stop

END Nome

Elim Checkpoint normally sheltered from north winds

Koyuk Once to Koyuk, the rest of the trail is over land

Nulato At confluence of Yukon and Nulato rivers

Galena Site of a former Air Force base

Safety Last checkpoint

Golovin Trail runs straight much of the way to White Mountain

Shaktoolik Trail crosses Norton Sound to Koyuk

Ruby Town of 185 is first checkpoint on Yukon River; first musher gets gourmet dinner

Norton Sound

Kaltag Mushers leave Yukon River at village of 230

Unalakleet The biggest town (population 747) between Anchorage and Nome and the first on Norton Sound

Cripple Abandoned mining town and race's halfway point; first musher gets $3,000

A L A S K A

River

100 km
100 miles

Ophir Ghost town

McGrath One of the larger towns (population 400) along the trail

Nikolai Village of about 100 people

Yukon

Takotna Pretty, welcoming village known for its fresh pies; favored spot to take 24-hour layover

Skwentna All mushers hit this checkpoint the first night of the race

Rohn Was an original Iditarod roadhouse for dog teams carrying mail; roadhouse is gone, replaced by a cabin built in the 1930s

Finger Lake

Rainy Pass The highest point on the trail

START Willow Race began March 2

Nome

ALASKA Area of detail

Anchorage

Yentna

Cook Inlet

Anchorage

1 You need a lot of courage to race across 1,500 miles (2,414 km) of snow and ice. You need skill to guide 16 sled dogs through the frozen rivers, forests, and mountains of Alaska. You need endurance[1] to make the 12-day trip from Anchorage to Nome. You need all of this, but you do not need to see.

2 Rachael Scdoris is the first legally blind sled dog racer, or musher, to compete in the Iditarod. In 2005, she made history when she crossed the finish line, taking 57th place out of 72 racers.

3 Since then, she has competed in the race three more times. She reached her dream, but not without facing a number of challenges.

4 Scdoris's dream began at a young age. She has been on a sled since she was three years old and has raced since she was 11. Her father, who raises sled dogs, has been her teacher and support. In 2005, at 19 years old, she was finally prepared to take on the Iditarod.

5 It would not be that easy, however. Scdoris has a rare disorder[2] that limits her vision. She cannot see details or colors. When Scdoris first applied for the Iditarod, she felt frustrated because the racing committee said no.

6 Says Scdoris, "My answer to people who question my ability is: 'Watch me.' I love my dogs, and I am competent[3] in every [part] of the sport, except that every now and then I need a little help seeing things out on the trail."

7 Eventually, Scdoris and her father persuaded the committee to let her race. They allowed Scdoris to have a visual guide. The guide rode behind her and told her by two-way radio if any danger was ahead.

8 The race was, in fact, one of the toughest in Iditarod history. Temperatures dropped to –52 degrees Fahrenheit (–47 degrees Centigrade) and winds blew over 60 miles (97 km) per hour. But Scdoris was determined[4] to meet the challenge. After 12 days, 10 hours, and 42 minutes, she led her dogs across the finish line.

9 Scdoris feels most comfortable and relaxed when racing. "My passion, the reason I believe I exist, is to raise, train, and race sled dogs," she says. "I am a musher, a sled dog racer, and I live for those moments when everything in the universe seems to align[5] into a delicate balance of perfection. In those moments my vision is never an issue."

10 Today, Scdoris has become an inspiration[6] for children and athletes alike, especially those who are disabled.[7] She is not embarrassed about her condition. She gives speeches around the world and repeats the same message: "If you have a passion for it, don't let people tell you you can't."

11 Many people told Scdoris she couldn't, but she has refused to give up. "Yes, I am legally blind," she says, "but blindness has not stopped me. In fact, it has barely slowed me down."

---

[1] **endurance:** the ability to remain strong and patient even though you feel pain or have problems

[2] **disorder:** a disease or illness that prevents part of the body from working correctly

[3] **competent:** having enough skill or knowledge to do something to a satisfactory standard

[4] **determined:** having a strong desire to continue to do something even when it is difficult

[5] **align:** to come together in an organized way and work well together

[6] **inspiration:** someone or something that encourages people to do or produce something good

[7] **disabled:** unable to use a part of the body properly

Building Word Knowledge

Using Participial Adjectives. When writers tell about an event in their own or someone else's life, they often describe people's feelings. In English, writers can use participial adjectives to reveal how someone is feeling. Participial adjectives can be formed by adding *-ed* to regular verbs. "Trust in the Snow" contains examples of participial adjectives that show how Rachael Scdoris felt.

Examples:

In 2005, at 19 years old, she was finally prepared to take on the Iditarod.

When Scdoris first applied for the Iditarod, she felt frustrated.

Reread the article on page 4 and find three more examples of participial adjectives that show how Scdoris was feeling. Circle the sentences and underline the participial adjectives.

Focused Practice

A. *Read the* **Tip for Writers.** *Then look back at your interview questions from Exercise B on page 3. Did the article answer your questions? Check (✓) "yes" or "no." If you check "yes," write Rachael's answer. The first one is done for you.*

	Answered?		Rachael's Answer
Who?	☑ yes	☐ no	*My father taught me to race sled dogs.*
What?	☐ yes	☐ no	
When?	☐ yes	☐ no	
Where?	☐ yes	☐ no	
Why?	☐ yes	☐ no	
How?	☐ yes	☐ no	

Tip for Writers

When you narrate a story, have questions in mind that you want to answer. Asking *wh-* **questions** (*who, what, when, where, why,* and *how*) will help you gather and include concrete information about the story you want to tell.

B. *Read the article again. Mark the statements* T *(true) or* F *(false).*

_____ **1.** The Iditarod takes place in Alaska.

_____ **2.** Rachael Scdoris was the first blind musher to compete in the Iditarod.

_____ **3.** Scdoris began racing at age three.

_____ **4.** Scdoris's mother taught her how to race sled dogs.

_____ **5.** Scdoris rode with another musher on her sled.

_____ **6.** It took Scdoris about 12 days to complete the Iditarod.

_____ **7.** Scdoris believes her blindness hurts her ability to race.

_____ **8.** Scdoris speaks to others about her disability.

C. *Read the statements. Check (✓) whether you agree or disagree with each statement. Discuss your answers with a partner.*

	Agree	Disagree
1. The Iditarod is a difficult race.	☐	☐
2. People with disabilities should be allowed to compete in the Iditarod.	☐	☐
3. It was unfair to let Rachael Scdoris use a visual guide.	☐	☐
4. Rachael Scdoris is a strong person.	☐	☐

D. *What physical challenges did Rachael Scdoris face? What emotional challenges did she face? How did Scdoris meet these challenges? Write a paragraph explaining the answers to these questions. Try to use one or two participial adjectives in your paragraph.*

Writing a Narrative Paragraph

In this unit, you are going to write a paragraph that tells a story. A narrative paragraph tells a story. It has a clear beginning and end. Sometimes the story is about an important time in someone's life—a time that changed the person in some way.

Like any paragraph, a narrative paragraph is a group of sentences that work together to express one main point, or controlling idea, about a topic. The sentences in a paragraph are organized in a logical way, for example, in time order or in order of importance.

A narrative paragraph has the same parts as other types of paragraphs: a topic sentence, body sentences, and one or more concluding sentences.

> **The Narrative Paragraph**
>
> ▶ Topic Sentence
> ▶ Body Sentences
> ▶ Concluding Sentence(s)

Step 1   Prewriting

Prewriting is an important step in the writing process. First, you choose your topic. Then you begin to think of ideas, gather information, and take notes. In this book, you will choose between two assignments. Then you will think of a specific topic and write about it.

For a narrative paragraph, choose a story that you can tell effectively in one paragraph. The story might be about a lesson or a surprising or scary event. It is better to write a paragraph about something specific, such as the first time you tried to do something new or difficult (for example, ride a horse or perform on stage) than it is to write about a topic that is too general or too large, such as your daily routine or a year in your life.

After choosing a topic, brainstorm questions you want to answer about the topic. The questions will help you gather ideas and information before you begin to write a first draft.

Your Own Writing

Choosing Your Assignment

A. *Choose Assignment 1 or Assignment 2.*

1. Tell a story about a time you or someone you know faced a challenge. What happened? What did you (or the person) do? For example, you might write a story about trying something new, such as learning a new language, playing a difficult game or sport, or traveling to a new place for the first time.

2. Tell a story about how a person or an animal helped someone overcome a physical or emotional challenge. For example, you might tell a story about how a teacher helped your best friend overcome her fear of public speaking. Or you might tell a story about how a dog helped a disabled veteran face his fears.

B. *Freewrite for 10 minutes about your assignment. Don't worry about grammar or spelling. Just write down all of the ideas that come into your mind. Here are some questions to get you started:*

• Why is the story one you want to tell?

• What was the most important moment in the story?

• In the end, how did you (or the person) feel about what happened?

• Did someone learn a lesson, feel surprised, or change in some way? If so, how?

C. Checking in. *Work with a partner who chose the same assignment. Discuss the ideas and details you just wrote. Ask your partner* who, what, when, where, why, *and* how *questions to find out more about his or her story. For example, did your partner . . .*

• explain who the story is about?

• tell what happened?

• describe where and when the story took place?

Share your opinions about your partner's story idea. Based on your discussion, make changes and additions to your writing.

D. *Complete the* wh- *questions chart. List the* wh- *questions your partner asked you on the left. Then write your answers on the right. There might be more than one question for each question word. Fill in as much information as you can. You will have a chance to review, change, or add information later in the unit.*

	Questions	Answers
Who?		
What?		
When?		
Where?		
Why?		
How?		

■ THE TOPIC SENTENCE

The topic sentence of a paragraph presents the topic and the controlling idea about it. The topic is who or what the paragraph is about. The controlling idea is the single point the writer is making about the topic. The controlling idea should be more than just a fact. It must be a specific viewpoint on the topic.

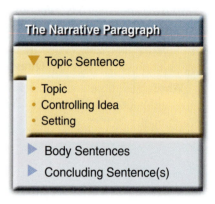

When you read the following sentences, you can see the difference between a factual statement and a controlling idea. The first sentence simply states a fact about Rachael Scdoris. The second sentence states a controlling idea about Rachael Scdoris: She is an inspiring role model for many people.

Examples:

Rachael Scdoris is legally blind. *(states a fact only)*

Rachael Scdoris's story of determination is an inspiration for many people. *(states a controlling idea)*

In a narrative paragraph, the topic sentence tells the topic *(who and/or what the story is about)*, the controlling idea *(what happened)*, and sometimes the setting *(where and when the story takes place)*. It usually comes at the beginning of the paragraph. Good writers try to make their topic sentences interesting so that readers will want to read on. Here are two examples of good topic sentences.

Examples:

In 2005, Rachael Scdoris faced a challenge that changed her life.

> **Topic:** A time when Rachael Scdoris faced a challenge
>
> **Controlling Idea:** Rachael Scdoris faced a challenge that changed her life.
>
> **Setting:** In 2005

Last summer when I was lost in the woods of Maine, I overcame my fear of the dark.

> **Topic:** A time when I was lost
>
> **Controlling Idea:** When I was lost, I overcame my fear of the dark.
>
> **Setting:** Last summer . . . in the woods of Maine

Focused Practice

A. *Read the topic sentences. Identify the topic* (who and/or what?), *the controlling idea* (what happened?), *and the setting* (where? when?). *Use your own words if necessary. The first one is done for you.*

1. Last week, my sister confronted her stage fright during her very first solo concert.

Topic: *My sister and her stage fright*

Controlling Idea: *My sister overcame her stage fright.*

Setting: *Last week; during her concert*

2. When my brother Victor moved from Vietnam to the United States in 2007, he had to overcome his fear of speaking with strangers.

Topic: _____

Controlling Idea: _____

Setting: _____

3. In kindergarten, my little brother had trouble learning to read, but his teacher didn't know it was because of his poor eyesight.

Topic: _____

Controlling Idea: _____

Setting: _____

4. When I was camping in Wyoming last year, I had a dangerous encounter with a bear that forced me to stay strong.

Topic: _____

Controlling Idea: _____

Setting: _____

B. *Read the following writing assignment and the sentences. Check (✓) the sentences that would make good topic sentences for the paragraph. Discuss your answers with a partner.*

Tell about a time when you or someone else faced a challenge.

_____ **1.** Helen was terrified of dogs until a hungry puppy came into her backyard.

_____ **2.** Last summer my aunt helped me get over my fear of being in the water.

_____ **3.** Mushers face a lot of challenges when they race.

_____ **4.** When I flew to Singapore last year, I learned the importance of staying calm.

_____ **5.** My little brother is good at all kinds of sports: soccer, basketball, and baseball.

_____ **6.** I faced a big challenge the day I interviewed for my first real job in New York.

_____ **7.** My best friend took a big risk on her 16th birthday.

_____ **8.** Until Yoko turned eight, she couldn't read because she had trouble telling left from right.

C. *Read the narrative paragraph. Choose the best topic sentence for the paragraph from the list below. Write it in the blank. Discuss your answer with a partner.*

Chipper

_____

_____

After her husband passed away, my grandmother stayed at home most of the time. She was heartbroken and lonely. A year later, my family decided to surprise her with a gift. Early in the morning, we went over to her house. In my hands, I held a cute brown puppy with tulip-shaped ears and a long tail. We had adopted him from a rescue shelter. My grandmother was sitting in her garden quietly reading a book when the puppy jumped out of my arms and ran over to her. Her face lit up. He jumped on her lap and began to lick her face. She couldn't stop laughing with delight. She gave each of us a big hug and tears came to her eyes. My grandmother decided to name the puppy Chipper because that is the way the little guy made her feel. Chipper is her new companion now, and he has encouraged her to spend more time out of the house. With Chipper by her side, my grandmother has learned that life can still be sweet and fulfilling even when you have suffered a big loss.

---

a. My grandmother and grandfather had been together for 55 years when he died.

b. My grandmother was very sad after my grandfather died two years ago.

c. When my grandmother lost her husband two years ago, a little gift helped her learn how to be happy again.

d. Chipper was a cute brown puppy that my family gave to my grandmother.

D. *Read the narrative paragraph. Write a topic sentence for the paragraph. Compare your sentence with your partner's. How are they the same? How are they different?*

The Jump of My Life

_____

_____

When my friends and I arrived in Banos, we wanted to take a tour of the mountains around the village. Early in the morning, we caught a small tour bus. While we

(continued)

---

were sightseeing, a local band was on the roof of the bus playing guitars and old wooden panpipes. The music put us in a festive mood. Eventually, the bus stopped on two bridges where people could practice swing jumping, an extreme sport that is very popular in Ecuador. I had always dreamed of doing something adventurous like that, so I decided to try it. I put on the helmet while an instructor locked the harness around my shoulders and legs. When I heard the clicking of the locks, I started to worry. My hands began to shake, and my heart started beating fast. After a few minutes, I forced myself to walk to the bridge, but I was too frightened to look over the edge. Finally, the instructor attached the bungee cord to my harness, and I knew it was too late to quit. "You can jump! You can do it!" my friends yelled from the other side of the bridge. I took a deep breath, opened my arms like a bird, and jumped. While I was falling, I felt scared, but once I began to swing and sail through the air, I felt exhilarated and free. My friends clapped and cheered. On that day falling through the air, I realized that doing something new and frightening can be a wonderful experience. I felt scared before the jump of my life, but much stronger because of it.

Your Own Writing

Planning Your Topic Sentence

A. *Write a draft of your topic sentence. First, list the topic, controlling idea, and setting. Introduce the story in an interesting way. Look back at your freewriting and* wh- *questions chart to help you.*

Topic: _____

Controlling Idea: _____

Setting: _____

Topic Sentence: _____

_____

B. Checking in. *Share your topic sentence with a partner. Did your partner . . .*

- present the topic and controlling idea in a clear and interesting way?
- tell where and when the story will take place?
- make you want to read on?

Tell your partner what you expect to find out in the story based on the topic sentence. Based on your partner's feedback, you may want to rewrite your topic sentence.

■ THE BODY SENTENCES

In the body of a paragraph, you develop and support the controlling idea you presented in your topic sentence. To develop and support the controlling idea of a narrative paragraph, you usually describe a sequence of events in time order. You also tell how the main character feels as the events occur. In most narrative paragraphs, there is a high point, or climax, toward the end of the story. The climax is the most important, exciting, or frightening moment in the story. It is often a turning point, after which the story changes in a big way.

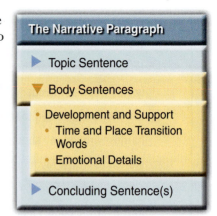

The key parts of a narrative paragraph are shown in the following paragraph.

Example:

Facing Stage Fright

Last week, my sister confronted her stage fright during her very first solo concert. Before her performance, she felt too scared to get on stage. She was prepared, but she was terrified of singing in front of a large audience. When it was her turn, she nervously walked across the stage to the microphone. After a few seconds, the music began. She closed her eyes, took a deep breath, and sang a Spanish folk song with such feeling that she moved the audience to tears. At the end of the performance, the audience applauded. My sister looked exhausted but relieved. With a smile, she stepped behind the curtain knowing she was no longer afraid of the stage.

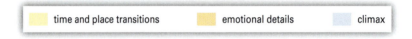

Putting Events in a Logical Order

Any paragraph you write must contain details to support the controlling idea. In a narrative paragraph, supporting details usually include information about the setting and characters. Just as you identified the setting and topic in your topic sentence, you have to include details about changes in time and place as the story continues. Writers often use prepositional phrases, such as the following, to express changes in time and place.

Prepositional Phrases of Time	Prepositional Phrases of Place
after that	on the bus/train/bicycle
at night	in the car
in the morning/afternoon/evening	on the road/sidewalk
for an hour	at school/home/the airport

Examples:

After a few minutes, I forced myself to walk to the bridge.

Eventually, the bus stopped on two bridges where people could practice swing jumping.

Early in the morning, we went over to see my grandmother at her house.

Focused Practice

A. *Complete the following paragraph with the prepositional phrases from the box to show changes in time and place. Add a capital letter if necessary when the phrase comes at the beginning of a sentence.*

after a few minutes	~~on that day~~	to a bench
during her first set	onto the tennis court	to the left side

Pushing through Pain

My sister Leah showed great courage last year during a tennis match at her local school. _____*On that day*_____, Leah was playing her final match of the season, so she really wanted to win. When she stepped _____, she looked confident and determined. _____ of games, she hit powerful serves and won six games, which was enough to win the set. She was very excited because she only needed to win one more set to be the winner. She continued playing powerfully and was winning again. Near the end of the second set, however, a terrible thing happened. She was running _____ of the court to hit the ball when her foot turned over to the side. She missed the ball and lost the game. She was very frustrated because she was only one game away from winning the match. She walked over _____ to sit down. She looked down at her ankle. Her coach said it was sprained. She looked hurt, exhausted, and upset. However, _____, she slowly stood up and walked back to the tennis court. She wasn't going to be discouraged. She was determined to succeed. She began playing, fought through her pain, and won the game, the set, and the match. Leah was thrilled to win, but more importantly, she was proud that she had the courage to push through her pain.

B. *Reread the paragraph "Pushing through Pain." Then discuss the questions with a partner.*

1. Underline the topic sentence. Who or what is the topic of the story, and where is the story set?

2. What kind of challenge does the main character face? Is it a physical or an emotional challenge, or both?

3. How do the character's feelings change during the story? Circle participial adjectives the writer uses to present emotional details.

4. What event marks the climax of the story? What emotion was the character feeling at this turning point in the story?

Including Emotional Details

In a narrative paragraph, you need to describe the emotional changes that your characters experience throughout the story. Emotional details will make your paragraph more exciting and suspenseful. In a narrative, the characters' feelings often get stronger as the story continues. Usually, the characters' strongest emotions occur during the climax of the story. The following sentences show examples of emotional details.

Examples:

The sounds of the instruments put us in a festive mood.

When I heard the click of the locks, I started to worry.

I was too frightened to look over the edge to see the water.

I felt exhilarated and free as I sailed through the air.

Focused Practice

Add an emotional detail to complete each sentence. Try to use some participial adjectives to show the character's emotions.

1. Rachael Scdoris felt _____ when she crossed the finish line.

2. When I stepped into the classroom on the first day of school, I was _____.

3. The skydiving instructor told me it was my turn to jump out of the plane, and I

   became very _____.

4. Joe was _____ when we couldn't understand what he was saying.

5. On the outside, I looked _____, but on the inside I felt _____.

6. I felt _____ when the rain stopped me from swimming in Lake Tahoe.

Your Own Writing

Finding Out More

A. *Learn more about the story you chose to write about, especially if your narrative is about someone else. Read the guidelines for researching a topic in the Appendix on pages 150–151.*

B. *Find out more details about the important parts of your story.*

- If you chose Assignment 1, ask questions about what happened when you or someone else faced a challenge. If you are writing about yourself, interview people who were there when the event occurred or talk to people who have had a similar experience.

- If you chose Assignment 2, find details about how the person or animal helped someone overcome a physical or emotional challenge. If you are writing about a person or animal you have heard about but don't know personally, such as a famous actor or athlete, find more information about his or her story online or at the library.

C. *Take notes on what you found out. For example, record answers to* **who, what, when, where, why,** *and* **how** *questions. You can add this information to the* **wh-** *questions chart on page 9. Use this information when you write your paragraph.*

D. Checking in. *Share your information with a partner. Did your partner . . .*

- gather enough details about the topic of the story?
- ask enough *wh-* questions about the topic?

Planning Your Body Sentences

A. *Before you begin writing the body sentences, complete the outline.*

- Copy your topic sentence from page 13.
- List the main events in time order.
- Add supporting details about what happened and how the characters felt.

Narrative Paragraph

Topic Sentence: _____

_____

▶ 1st Event: _____

   ▶ Detail: _____

▶ 2nd Event: _____

   ▶ Detail: _____

▶ 3rd Event: _____

   ▶ Detail: _____

▶ 4th Event: _____

   ▶ Detail: _____

▶ 5th Event: _____

   ▶ Detail: _____

B. Checking in. *Share your outline with a partner. Tell your partner whether . . .*

- the story has a clear beginning and ending.
- one event marks the climax or turning point.
- there are enough details about changes in setting and the main character's feelings.

Based on your partner's feedback, you may want to rewrite parts of your outline.

■ THE CONCLUDING SENTENCE(S)

The concluding sentences are where you wrap up or close your paragraph. Writers usually return to the controlling idea they expressed in the topic sentence and say it in different words. They often signal the end of the story with a prepositional phrase of time such as *on that day*, *after that experience*, or *in the end*.

There are many ways to end a narrative paragraph. You might express a final thought about the story, such as your opinion about what happened. You might explain a lesson the main character learned, or you might describe how the character's attitude or beliefs changed as a result of the experience.

The following are three strategies you might want to use to end your narrative paragraph about facing a challenge or difficult situation:

The Narrative Paragraph

▶ Topic Sentence
▶ Body Sentences
▼ Concluding Sentence(s)
  • Restated Controlling Idea
  • Final Thoughts
  • Lesson Learned

1. Express a surprising thought that occurred because of the experience.

2. Describe how the experience made you or someone else think in a new way.

3. Explain how the experience taught a lesson or caused someone to change.

Examples:

My sister was thrilled to win, but more importantly, she was proud that she had the courage to push past her pain.

On that day falling through the air, I realized that doing something new and frightening can be a wonderful experience. I felt scared before the jump of my life, but much stronger because of it.

With Chipper by her side, my grandmother has learned that life can still be sweet and fulfilling even when you have suffered a big loss.

Focused Practice

Read the paragraph. Answer the questions on page 19 about the concluding sentences.

To the Rescue

I felt like a hero the morning I saved my mother from an unwanted guest in our house. It was early in the morning before school. My mother was making breakfast in the kitchen when I woke up and went downstairs to join her. I got myself some juice and sat down. While I was wishing that I was still in bed, all of sudden I heard my mother scream, "Bug! Bug! Get it! Quick!" She was so scared. I looked down at the kitchen floor and saw a long black millipede crawling under her feet. I was a little scared too, but I overcame my fear because I wanted to help my mom. The millipede scurried away from me quickly. I stepped on it, but it didn't die. It just kept running. While I was chasing it, my mother was standing on a chair on the other side of the room still screaming. After a couple minutes, I trapped the creature in a corner. I picked it up with a napkin and threw it outside as fast as I could. Once it was gone, my mother stepped down from the chair and gave me a big hug and kiss. "Thank you, honey," she said. We both felt relieved that the millipede was finally gone. I was proud that I could be my mother's hero on that morning. I was also surprised that my mother was so scared of that little bug. She is a strong woman, but not when it comes to bugs!

1. Underline the sentence that returns to the controlling idea of the topic sentence.

2. What prepositional phrase of time does the writer use to let you know the story is ending? Circle it.

3. What strategies does the writer use to close the essay? _____

Your Own Writing

Planning Your Conclusion

A. *How will you rephrase your controlling idea in a concluding sentence? List your ideas here.*

_____

_____

B. *What strategy will you use to close the paragraph?*

_____

C. **Checking in.** *Share your ideas with a partner. Did your partner . . .*

- figure out an interesting way to return to his or her controlling idea?
- choose an effective concluding strategy?

Writing Your First Draft

Read the Tip for Writers. *Review your notes on pages 9, 13, and 17. Then write the first draft of your paragraph. When you are finished, give your paragraph a working title. Hand in your draft to your teacher.*

Tip for Writers

When you write your first draft, ask yourself if you have all the necessary parts. Use *who, what, when, where, why,* and *how* questions to help you include enough information.

Revising your work is an essential part of the writing process. This is your opportunity to be sure that your paragraph has all the important pieces and that it is clear.

Focused Practice

A. *Read the narrative paragraph.*

Zipping Along

Two years ago, I faced a big challenge on a trip to Monteverde, Costa Rica, with my friends. My friends asked me to go zip-lining, where people fly through the jungle on a long wire. I was interested, but it also made me nervous. When I woke up in the morning, I felt a little worried. When we got to the site, there was dense fog in the air. The jungle looked mysterious. We walked across a long bridge through the mist, and it felt as if we were floating in air. Then I saw the zip line, and I got scared. It was long, and it disappeared far away into the jungle. When it was my turn, a man hooked me up to the line, and I stepped onto the edge of the platform. My heart was racing and my hands were sweating. I was so high above the forest floor. I told myself to calm down. I took a deep breath and stepped off. I began to fall, and the wind was blowing on my face. I was terrified. I screamed as I went faster and faster through the jungle. Then an amazing thing happened. I opened my eyes, and I felt as free as a bird. I was surprised that I was actually doing it. I was flying! When I got to the other side, I did not want it to end. On that day, I learned that when I face a challenge, I just need to take a deep breath and enjoy the moment.

B. *Work with a partner. Answer the questions about the paragraph.*

   1. What is the controlling idea of the paragraph? Underline the words that state it.

   2. What is the setting? Circle the words in the topic sentence that tell you.

   3. What words does the writer use to present emotional details about the main character? Check (✓) participial adjectives that explain how the character feels.

   4. What event marks the climax or turning point of the story? Put a star at the beginning of the sentence that describes this event.

   5. What strategy does the writer use to wrap up or close the story? _____

C. Checking in. *Discuss your marked-up paragraph with another pair of students. Then in your group, share one thing about the paragraph that you found the most interesting.*

Building Word Knowledge

The writer included participial adjectives in "Zipping Along" to express the characters' feelings, including *interested*, *worried*, and *surprised*.

Work with a partner. Write five sentences using some of the participial adjectives from the box. Describe the feelings of the characters in your story. An example is done for you.

confused	discouraged	excited	satisfied
determined	embarrassed	frightened	surprised

1. *On the first day of school, my brother was frightened.*

2. _____

3. _____

4. _____

5. _____

6. _____

Your Own Writing

Revising Your Draft

A. *Reread the first draft of your paragraph. Use the Revision Checklist to identify parts of your writing that might need improvement.*

B. *Review your plans and notes and your responses to the Revision Checklist. Then revise your first draft. Save your revised paragraph. You will look at it again in the next section.*

Revision Checklist

Did you . . .

☐ express the topic, setting, and controlling idea in your topic sentence?

☐ describe the events in time order, including the climax or turning point?

☐ include enough details about the setting, characters, and emotions?

☐ use prepositional phrases to express changes in time and setting?

☐ restate the controlling idea in your concluding sentences?

☐ use an effective concluding strategy?

☐ use any participial adjectives in your story?

☐ give your paragraph a good title?

■ GRAMMAR PRESENTATION

Before you hand in your revised paragraph, you must check it for any errors in grammar, punctuation, and spelling. In this section, you will learn about the past progressive and the simple past. You will focus on this grammar when you edit and proofread your paragraph.

Past Progressive and Simple Past

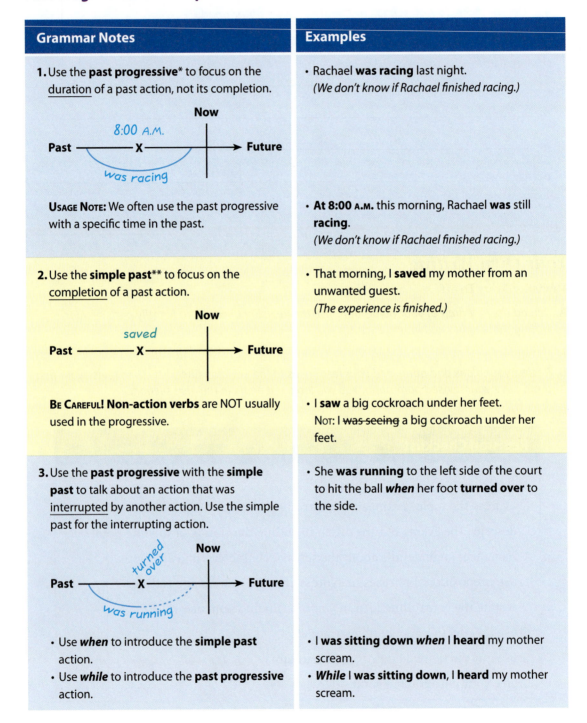

Grammar Notes	Examples
1. Use the **past progressive*** to focus on the <u>duration</u> of a past action, not its completion. **USAGE NOTE:** We often use the past progressive with a specific time in the past.	• Rachael **was racing** last night. *(We don't know if Rachael finished racing.)* • **At 8:00 A.M.** this morning, Rachael **was** still **racing**. *(We don't know if Rachael finished racing.)*
2. Use the **simple past**** to focus on the <u>completion</u> of a past action. **BE CAREFUL!** **Non-action verbs** are NOT usually used in the progressive.	• That morning, I **saved** my mother from an unwanted guest. *(The experience is finished.)* • I **saw** a big cockroach under her feet. NOT: I ~~was seeing~~ a big cockroach under her feet.
3. Use the **past progressive** with the **simple past** to talk about an action that was <u>interrupted</u> by another action. Use the simple past for the interrupting action. • Use *when* to introduce the **simple past** action. • Use *while* to introduce the **past progressive** action.	• She **was running** to the left side of the court to hit the ball *when* her foot **turned over** to the side. • I **was sitting down** *when* I **heard** my mother scream. • *While* I **was sitting down**, I **heard** my mother scream.

4. Use the **past progressive** with *while* to talk about two or more actions in progress at the same time in the past. Use the past progressive in both clauses.

- A local band **was playing** music *while* we **were sightseeing**.

  OR
- *While* we **were sightseeing**, a local band **was playing** music.

5. BE CAREFUL! A sentence with both clauses in the simple past has a very <u>different meaning</u> from a sentence with one clause in the simple past and one clause in the past progressive.

a. Both clauses in the **simple past**:

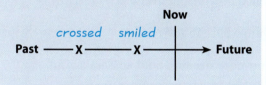

- When Rachael **crossed** the finish line, she **smiled**.

  (*First, she crossed the finish line; then she smiled.*)

b. One clause in the **simple past**, the other in the **past progressive**:

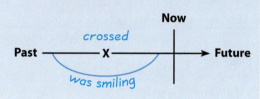

- When Rachael **crossed** the finish line, she **was smiling**.

  (*First, she was smiling; then she crossed the finish line.*)

---

* The past progressive is formed by adding *was/were* and *-ing* to the base form of a verb.

** The simple past is formed by adding *-d* or *-ed* to the base form of a verb.

Focused Practice

A. *Read each sentence. Circle the correct word or words.*

1. As a young boy, I (**loved / was loving**) to climb trees.

2. My friends and I often (**climbed / were climbing**) trees after school.

3. One day, while we (**walked / were walking**) home from school, we

   (**saw / were seeing**) an enormous old oak tree.

4. We (**ran / were running**) to the tree and (**started / were starting**) to climb it.

5. While we (**raced / were racing**) each other to the top, I (**scraped / was scraping**) my hand on a rough branch.

6. When we finally (**made / were making**) it to the top, we (**felt / were feeling**) victorious.

7. I will never forget the day we (**conquered / were conquering**) that old oak tree.

B. *Read each sentence. Underline the verbs in the simple past. If necessary, change any verbs to the past progressive to make the meaning clearer. The first two are done for you.*

1. When I <u>was</u> 11 years old, I <u>had</u> a strange experience with a spider.

    was sleeping
2. It <u>happened</u> while I <u>slept</u> in my bed.

3. That night, I felt very tired, so I went straight to bed after dinner.

4. I put my head on the pillow, fell asleep quickly, and started dreaming.

5. I dreamed that a brown spider crawled up my leg, so I slapped myself hard.

6. When I woke up, I screamed and tried to shake the spider off my leg.

7. My mom walked in while I jumped around in my bed.

8. Then she turned on the light, and I calmed down right away.

9. I realized that no spider was on me or anywhere in the room.

10. I went back to sleep, but I told myself never to dream about spiders again!

C. *Complete the paragraph with the correct form of the verbs in parentheses. Use the simple past or past progressive. Some items have more than one correct answer.*

Driven to Succeed

Seven years ago, I _____*had*_____ a difficult time when I
        1. (have)

_____ my driver's license test in the United States. I
   2. (take)

_____ intimidated about driving in the United States because
   3. (feel)

people's driving habits _____ so different than in my country, Vietnam.
        4. (be)

First, I _____ the driving laws and _____ them to
   5. (study)   **6. (use)**

practice driving. Then on the day of the test, I _____ to the testing
        7. (go)

center. When the instructor _____ next to me, I _____
     8. (sit)   **9. (feel)**

shy because I did not know her. While I _____ the car, my hands
       10. (drive)

_____ and _____, but I _____
 11. (sweat)   **12. (shake)**   **13. (tell)**

myself to be confident. I _____ that I could do it. Luckily, the
   14. (know)

(continued)

---

instructor _____ 15. (be) easygoing and friendly. I _____ 16. (finish)
my test, and I _____ 17. (pass) ! I _____ 18. (smile) when the woman
_____ 19. (hand) me my U.S. driver's license. That day, I _____ 20. (learn)
a great lesson—to have more confidence in myself and my abilities.

D. *Write five sentences related to the topic you chose on page 8. Use the* simple past *and* past progressive. *These may be sentences you already have in your paragraph.*

1. _____

_____

2. _____

_____

3. _____

_____

4. _____

_____

5. _____

_____

Your Own Writing

Editing Your Draft

A. *Use the Editing Checklist to edit and proofread your paragraph.*

B. *Prepare a clean copy of the final draft of your paragraph and hand it in to your teacher.*

Editing Checklist

Did you . . .

☐ include the simple past and past progressive and use them correctly?

☐ use correct verb forms, punctuation, and spelling?

☐ use participial adjectives and other words correctly?

UNIT 2 Branded for Success

IN THIS UNIT   You will be writing a descriptive paragraph about a favorite business, product, or logo.

Many successful businesses use a logo, or striking symbol, to brand or create an image of themselves. Think of some of the well-known logos you see every day—for example, the colorful Google logo you see when you do an online search or the Nike logo you see on famous sports stars' T-shirts and shoes. What logos do you recognize right away? Are you loyal to any brands? If so, which ones and why are you loyal to them?

Planning for Writing

■ BRAINSTORM

A. *Work with a partner. Look at the store photo. Then discuss the following questions.*

1. What kind of store is this?

2. What kinds of people shop here?

3. What kind of music do you think this store should play while customers shop? Why?

B. Using a Descriptive Web. When you are gathering information about a topic, you can use a descriptive web to think of and record ideas and descriptive details.

With your partner, select one of the logos below. Write the name of the company in the central oval on the descriptive web. Then use each of the outer ovals to give information about the company's logo. Use these questions to help you brainstorm information.

1. What company does the logo stand for?

2. What does the logo look like? For example, what color is it and how is it shaped?

3. What do you think the logo means? Why do you think the company uses this logo?

4. In your opinion, is it a successful way for the company to brand itself?

Muzak for the Masses[1]

1   What does chocolate sound like? What sound do summer dresses make? You might not think of food and clothing in terms of sounds, but the company Muzak makes it its business to do just that.

2   Muzak describes its purpose simply: to bring "the emotion and energy of [a] business to life in song." The company creates soundscapes, or groups of songs, that successfully fit the image of a specific business.

3   When you hear music playing in a grocery or clothing store, there is a good chance you are listening to a Muzak soundscape. Muzak soundscapes are not just background music, however. Stores that use them hope the music will motivate their customers to spend more money.

4   Muzak calls its creative process "audio architecture." Just as architects can turn a drawing into a building, Muzak's "music architects" can build soundscapes that help sell a company's brand and products.

5   Muzak asks each of its clients[2] the same questions: *What is your company like? What do you want to sell? Who are your customers? How do you want them to feel?*

6   With this information, Muzak creates soundscapes that make customers comfortable enough to stay longer at a restaurant or happy enough to spend more time shopping for clothes.

7   Says the company, "When you employ the science of Muzak, workers tend to get more done, more efficiently and feel happier … In a store, people seem to shop in a more relaxed and leisurely manner. In a bank, customers are generally more calm; tellers and other personnel are more efficient.[3] In general, people feel better about where they are, whether it's during work or leisure time."

8   Research studies have shown that music can affect people's buying habits. Upbeat[4] music can make customers at a fast-food restaurant leave sooner—that's good for business. In contrast, romantic music can make couples spend more time at a fine restaurant. This might lead to dessert or an after-dinner drink, and more money for the restaurant.

9   The key to the success of a Muzak soundscape is both the type of songs that are played and the way the songs are arranged. The songs must "tell the story" of the business so that customers feel the emotional connection between the songs and the store. They must also sound natural and pleasing together.

10   A hip teenage clothing store needs music that sounds as if you are at a party or club. The songs should have a quick beat and no silence[5] between them.

11   A high-end fashion boutique[6] needs a different kind of soundscape. Shoppers must be made to feel positive and comfortable, so no loud music or bad words are allowed. The songs should fade in and out with a tiny silence, or space, between them to create a more easygoing atmosphere. During the silences, a shopper might be more likely to look at different clothes on another rack. When closing time comes, the music might speed up to put tired customers in a better mood for last-minute shopping.

12   The people at Muzak have even thought about what the sound system should look like. When you walk into a youth clothing store, the speakers are in your face.[7] They look loud and active, just like teenagers. In a candle shop, the mood is calm, dark, and soothing. Customers can't see the speakers—they can only feel the music.

13   Muzak is in the business of selling emotion through sound, and it has satisfied hundreds of successful companies, from hotels to airports to hospitals. More than 100 million people hear Muzak each day as they go about their daily lives. And the songs never get old. Muzak has over 1.5 million to choose from, with 15,000 new songs added every month.

14   Muzak has come a long way in its 75-year history. When the company began, it was known only for producing "elevator music"—the kind of soft, boring music you sometimes hear when you call a bank and are put on hold. People used to laugh at Muzak, but not now. Today, it has succeeded in becoming the leader in making background music for the masses—and money for businesses.

---

[1] **the masses:** all the ordinary people in a society
[2] **clients:** people who pay a person or organization for a service
[3] **efficient:** working well, quickly, and without wasting time, money, or energy
[4] **upbeat:** cheerful and making you feel good
[5] **silence:** absence of sound or noise
[6] **boutique:** a small store that sells very fashionable clothes or decorations
[7] **in your face:** direct and often shocking or surprising

Building Word Knowledge

Using Word Forms. When you write, be sure to use the correct form of each word. Many English words have a variety of forms, including noun (n.), verb (v.), adjective (adj.), and adverb (adv.) forms.

Locate the forms of the word succeed *in "Muzak for the Masses." Add them to the word forms chart. The first one is done for you.*

Verb	Noun	Adjective	Adverb
1. *has succeeded*	2.	3.	4.

Focused Practice

A. *Circle the letter of the correct answer to each question.*

1. What is Muzak's main purpose?

   a. to collect over 1.5 million songs

   b. to create soundscapes for businesses

   c. to keep its customers happy

2. What do music architects do?

   a. They turn a drawing into a building.

   b. They build song lists for businesses.

   c. They ask clients who their customers are.

3. What affects the flow in a Muzak soundscape?

   a. how songs speed up during closing time

   b. how songs make a store feel like a club

   c. how songs connect to each other

4. How many people listen to Muzak per day?

   a. 100 million

   b. 1.5 million

   c. 15,000

5. Why is Muzak successful today?

   a. It has become the leader in making background music for businesses.

   b. It is known mostly for making elevator music.

   c. It asks its clients the same questions about their companies.

B. *According to the article, what type of music environment would best match each of the following businesses? Write the letter of the correct answer.*

_____ **1.** a fast-food restaurant

_____ **2.** a fine restaurant

_____ **3.** a high-end fashion boutique

_____ **4.** a youth clothing store

_____ **5.** a candle shop

a. romantic music

b. speakers that are visible on the walls

c. speakers that are hidden

d. songs that fade in and out

e. upbeat music

C. *Read the* Tip for Writers *and the example. Then complete the* when *clauses. Look back at the reading to finish each sentence. Discuss your answers with a partner.*

Tip for Writers

Writers often use the conjunction **when** to show how two ideas connect to each another. *When* can mean "at the same time" or "after" depending on the context. Combining sentences with *when* can make transitions between ideas clearer. If *when* appears at the beginning of a sentence, a comma is placed between the two clauses.

Example:

When people hear music playing in a grocery store, they are probably listening to a Muzak soundtrack.

   1. When businesses employ the science of Muzak,

   _____.

   2. When fast-food restaurants play upbeat music,

   _____.

   3. When a store is about to close, _____.

   4. When you walk into a youth clothing store, _____.

   5. When Muzak first began, _____.

D. *What type of music might match the feel of your favorite store? Write a short paragraph in which you describe the type of music and explain why it is linked in your mind to the store and its products. Try to use the conjunction* when *in your paragraph.*

_____

_____

_____

_____

_____

_____

_____

_____

_____

Writing a Descriptive Paragraph

In this unit, you are going to write a descriptive paragraph about a favorite business, product, or logo. A descriptive paragraph can be about any person, place, or thing. In order to paint a clear picture of a topic, a descriptive paragraph often contains descriptive details to show readers what something looks, sounds, feels, tastes, or smells like. It may also describe how something makes you feel, what its key characteristics are, or what impression it creates in other people. In addition, a descriptive paragraph may include some background information to explain *who, what, when, where, why,* and *how*.

> **The Descriptive Paragraph**
> ▶ Topic Sentence
> ▶ Body Sentences
> ▶ Concluding Sentence(s)

A descriptive paragraph has the same parts as all paragraphs: a topic sentence, body sentences, and one or more concluding sentences. Later you will learn more about how a descriptive paragraph differs from other paragraphs.

Step 1   Prewriting

When you write a descriptive paragraph, the first prewriting step is to select a topic that you can describe easily in a single paragraph. If you choose a topic that you can picture clearly in your mind, writing a description of it will be easier.

Once you have selected a topic, use a graphic organizer to gather and arrange descriptive information before you begin to write a first draft.

Your Own Writing

Choosing Your Assignment

A. *Choose Assignment 1 or Assignment 2.*

  1. Describe a favorite business, for example, a store, a hotel, a company, or a restaurant. The business should be a specific one that you like for specific reasons.

  2. Describe one of your favorite products or logos. The product could be something you bought recently. The logo could be one that appeals to you for specific reasons and has made you like a specific brand.

B. *Freewrite for 10 minutes about your assignment. Here are some questions to get you started:*

  • Why is this business, product, or logo a favorite?

  • What descriptive details (for example, details about how it looks, sounds, feels, tastes, or smells) can you think of in connection with your topic?

  • What key features or characteristics does your topic have?

  • What additional information (*who, what, when, where, why,* and *how*) might help you present a clear picture of your topic? ➡

C. Checking in. *Work with a partner who chose the same assignment. Discuss the ideas and details you just wrote. Did your partner give descriptive details about how the business, product, or logo . . .*

- looks, sounds, or feels?

- makes a lasting impression?

- is worth liking or buying?

Share your opinions about your partner's topic. Based on your discussion, make changes and additions to your writing.

D. *Complete the descriptive web. List key features, descriptive details, and other information about your topic. Fill in as much information as you can. You will have a chance to review, change, or add information later in the unit.*

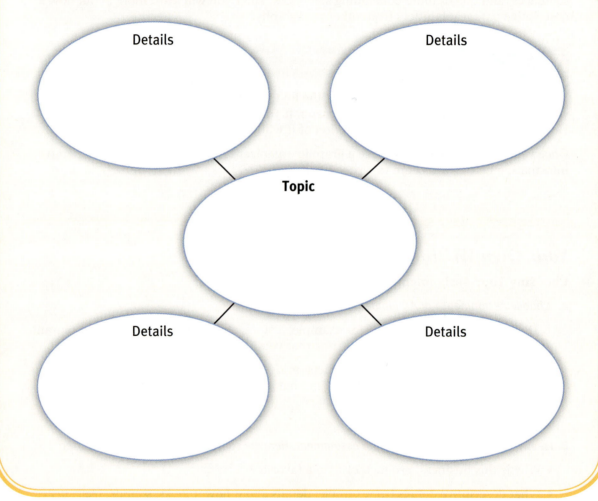

THE TOPIC SENTENCE

In a descriptive paragraph, the topic sentence identifies the topic (the person, place, or thing your description is about) and your controlling idea about the topic (the opinion or observation that you will develop and support with descriptive details). It may also include one or more concrete descriptive words that help express your controlling idea about the topic.

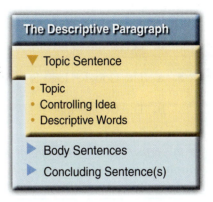

When you read the following topic sentences for a descriptive paragraph, you can see the differences between a strong topic sentence and a weak one. The first three sentences have concrete descriptive words, but the last two do not. In the final two sentences, the words *great* and *good* are too general. They don't show the reader "why" the logo or brand is a favorite.

Examples:

	topic	controlling idea and descriptive words

Strong: Muzak's soundscapes have become very successful by creating emotion through music.

Strong: Hotel Vitale is my favorite place to stay because of its calming, natural atmosphere.

Strong: Pret a Manger is my favorite place to eat because it serves fresh food at a low price.

Weak: Google's logo is great, and it is my favorite. *(not specific; doesn't describe why it's great)*

Weak: Buttercup Bakery makes good cupcakes, so it is my favorite brand. *(not specific; doesn't describe what's good about them)*

Focused Practice

A. *Read the following writing assignment. Then read each pair of topic sentences. Circle the strong topic sentence in each pair. Discuss your answers with a partner.*

Describe a successful product or logo.

1. **a.** I think Trek® bicycles are the best because they are both long-lasting and stylish.

   b. I have owned many bicycles, but my Trek bicycle will always be my favorite.

2. **a.** The prancing horse on the Ferrari logo is an exciting and effective way to express speed.

   b. I like the Ferrari logo a great deal because this brand of car is my favorite.

(continued)

3. **a.** The Starbucks Coffee® logo is recognized by people all around the world.

     b. The Starbucks Coffee logo has international appeal because it looks friendly and exotic.

4. **a.** Levi's® are my favorite type of jeans because they fit well and look modern.

     b. Levi's makes great jeans that I like to wear at school, at home, and even at work.

5. **a.** The Google® logo is very popular and many people like it.

     b. The Google logo is successful because it is colorful and versatile.

B. *Read the descriptive paragraph and the topic sentences on page 35. Circle the letter of the best topic sentence for the paragraph. Then write the sentence in the blank.*

The Bitten Apple

_____

_____

Ever since 1977, Apple has used a very simple logo. What could be more basic and recognizable than the simple shape of an apple? Just in case anyone might confuse the apple with a tomato, the apple logo has a "bite" taken out of its top right corner. The original 1977 Apple logo had horizontal, rainbow-colored stripes. These colors looked handsome and inviting on the early Apple computers, which had small screens. When Apple began making more streamlined products with large glass screens, such as the iPhone, iPad, and iTouch, the company changed the logo's color to fit the look of its newer products. In 1999, Apple stopped using its rainbow logo. Ever since that time, the bitten apple shape has been a single color. Sometimes it has been red, blue, or gray. One of the most recent versions of the logo is a silvery and slightly transparent color that looks a lot like glass. It matches the silvery chrome color of many of Apple's most recent computers. I like the silvery logo best. It still has the simplicity of the original bitten apple shape, but it is also more subtle and modern than the rainbow logo that Apple used years ago. In conclusion, Apple's latest logo appeals to me and countless others because it combines a basic shape with a fresh, modern look.

---

a. Apple has been making computers for more than 35 years and is a very successful company.

b. The new silvery Apple logo is really cool-looking, and I like it.

c. I have owned an Apple computer for several years, and I like the company's logo.

d. Like many people, I find Apple's logo very appealing because it is simple but modern.

C. *Read the descriptive paragraph. In pairs or small groups, write a topic sentence for the paragraph.*

Muji

_____

_____

Muji is a retail store in Japan that sells basic products such as food, clothing, and stationery. The first Muji store opened in Tokyo, but today Muji has stores all over the world. Muji uses cheap, simple packaging that doesn't hurt people's eyes with loud colors or bright pictures. Most items are wrapped in simple clear plastic or brown paper. The company also has a simple "no-brand" policy that I like and respect. There is no official logo, and there is very little advertising. People learn about Muji by word-of-mouth, or hearing about the store from a friend. As a result, people focus on the products instead of the name of the company. The name *Muji* (meaning "no brand, good product") reflects the company's belief in simple, sound products. When shoppers buy a Muji T-shirt, there is no logo on it; instead, the shirt has a blank rubber square on the front, where people can design their own logos. Even without a logo, Muji has become very successful. All in all, I like Muji's products and appreciate the company's focus on simplicity. As a result of its no-brand policy, I think Muji has successfully made something out of nothing.

Your Own Writing

Finding Out More

A. *Learn more about the topic you chose to write about, especially if there is an interesting history behind the business, product, or logo.*

- Go online or to the library to locate at least three sources that contain background information and descriptive details about your topic.

- Search for or look up the name of your business, product, or logo—for example, search under keywords such as *BlackBerry phones*, *Starbucks stores*, or *the Ferrari logo*.

- Keep these questions in mind as you research your topic: *What does the business or product do? Why is/was it successful? What are its special characteristics?*

B. *Take notes on what you found out. List important facts and supporting details about your topic. Note interesting descriptive details that will make your description come alive. Add this information to your descriptive web on page 32. Use this information when you write your paragraph. Be sure to note the sources for your information. (See the Appendix on pages 150–151.)*

C. **Checking in.** *Share your information with a partner. Did your partner . . .*

- gather enough background information and descriptive details about the topic?

- ask and answer enough *who, what, when, where, why,* and *how* questions about the topic?

Planning Your Topic Sentence

A. *Write a draft of your topic sentence. First, list the topic, controlling idea, and one or more descriptive words. Remember: Your topic sentence should suggest an idea or observation that you will prove in your paragraph. Look back at your freewriting and descriptive web to help you.*

Topic: _____

Controlling Idea about the Topic: _____

Descriptive Word(s): _____

Topic Sentence: _____

_____

B. **Checking in.** *Share your topic sentence with a partner. Did your partner . . .*

- present the topic and controlling idea in a clear and engaging way?

- introduce specific descriptive information about the topic?

- make you want to read on?

Tell your partner what you expect to learn about the topic based on the topic sentence. Based on your partner's feedback, you may want to rewrite your topic sentence.

■ THE BODY SENTENCES

In the body of a descriptive paragraph, you support and develop your topic by giving background information and descriptive details.

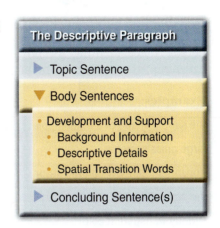

The Descriptive Paragraph

▶ Topic Sentence

▼ Body Sentences

- Development and Support
- Background Information
- Descriptive Details
- Spatial Transition Words

▶ Concluding Sentence(s)

Giving Background Information

Before you describe your topic, you usually explain who or what you are describing. This background information may include a short history of the topic, such as who a person is, what a company or organization does, where a place is located, or when an event happened, as shown in the exampes below.

Examples:

Who is it?   What does it do?
Muji is a retail store in Japan that sells basic products such as food, clothing, and stationery.

Where is it located?   When did it begin?
The first Muji store opened in Tokyo in 1983, but today it has stores all over the world.

Background information often comes after the topic sentence when it explains the history of the person or object you describe. When you describe the history of someone or something, present the information in a clear sequence. For example, you might present the steps involved in how something works or describe the order in which something happened. When you reread the sentences about Apple's logo below you will notice that the writer has presented information in the order in which it occurred, that is, in time order.

Example:

I like Apple's logo because it is simple and modern. The logo has always used the simple shape of a bitten apple, but Apple has changed its colors to keep it looking new and fresh. The original 1977 logo was multicolored. However, Apple has recently been making more products that feature large glass screens, such as the iPhone, iPad, and iTouch. Therefore, the newest logo fits the image of Apple's products today.

Including and Arranging Descriptive Details

Descriptive details help you create a picture of what something or someone is like and how something happens or works. Writers often use adjectives to help readers picture a person, place, or thing. As shown in the following examples, adjectives give details about age, color, size, material, and shape.

Examples:

the simple shape of a bitten apple

large glass screens

horizontal, rainbow-colored stripes

the newest logo

slightly transparent color

clear plastic or brown paper

There are many different ways to organize descriptive details in a paragraph. If you are describing an object or place, you can use spatial order phrases (for example, *left to right, near to far, top to bottom,* or *front to back*). In Unit 1, you learned how to use prepositional phrases to show changes in time and place in a narrative. You can also use prepositional phrases to put descriptive details into spatial order in a paragraph.

Example:

When I enter a Muji store, I can always find what I want. The layout of the Muji store near my house in London helps me shop in a peaceful and organized way. On the left side of the store, there are storage items, such as brown handwoven baskets and clear plastic containers. Small tables hold paper, cards, and envelopes in the center of the store, and on the right side, I can find items for the kitchen, such as pot holders and dish towels.

Another way to organize descriptive details is to group similar details together; for example, all the details about the color of an object are presented together followed by all the details about its shape, as shown below.

Example:

The logo is silver to match the color of many of Apple's computers. Silver feels more modern than the colorful logo that Apple used before. The shape of the apple is unique because there is a "bite" taken out of the top. Without the bite, the apple would look more like a tomato; the bite helps people recognize the Apple brand.

| color | shape |

Focused Practice

A. *Read the topic sentence. Which body sentences give background information about the topic? Write* B *next to those sentences. Which body sentences give specific descriptive details about the topic? Write* D *next to those sentences.*

Topic Sentence: Hotel Vitale is my favorite place to stay because of its calming, natural atmosphere.

_____ **1.** This luxury hotel is located in San Francisco, California.

_____ **2.** It is on the San Francisco Bay.

_____ **3.** The rooms contain large windows that let a lot of bright sunlight in.

_____ **4.** Lit-up river stones sit on bedside tables in each room.

_____ **5.** Fresh lavender above the doors fills the rooms with a beautiful, fresh scent.

B. *Read the following paragraph. Then check (✓) the questions that the paragraph answers with descriptive details. Compare your answers with a partner's.*

> ### Hotel Vitale
>
> Hotel Vitale is my favorite place to stay because of its extremely calming, natural atmosphere. This luxury hotel is located in San Francisco, California, on the San Francisco Bay. The hotel achieves its "luxury, naturally" image through the use of natural elements and soothing music. The rooms contain large windows that let in a lot of bright sunlight and allow guests to look out at the water. Natural materials such as wood and stone are used throughout the hotel, and lit-up river stones sit on the bedside tables in each room. Fresh lavender above the doors fills the rooms with a beautiful, fresh scent. Hotel Vitale completes its natural image with a Muzak soundtrack that features calming instrumental music in the lobby and livelier music in the lounge. When guests enjoy the hotel's hot spas on the roof deck and listen to peaceful music, they feel as if they are in paradise. Hotel Vitale has succeeded in creating a powerful yet calming energy through its design. This hotel is more than just a place to stay; it is an unforgettable experience.

_____ **1.** What is the hotel's image?

_____ **2.** What is the view like from the rooms?

_____ **3.** How many rooms does the hotel have?

_____ **4.** What natural materials are used?

_____ **5.** What color is the lobby?

(continued)

_____ **6.** How do the rooms smell?

_____ **7.** What kind of music is in the lobby?

_____ **8.** What music does the lounge play?

_____ **9.** How much does a room cost?

_____ **10.** How popular is the hotel?

C. *Put the sentences in order from 1 to 5 to make a paragraph with a topic sentence, background information, and descriptive details. Compare your answers with a partner's.*

_____ My Jeep has a big, tough look. It has a strong, boxy frame. Also, the wheels are large, so it can handle off-road driving on dirt roads.

_____ I got my Jeep when I was in high school. My parents bought it for me after I got my driver's license.

_____ My Jeep is one of my favorite possessions because it is rugged and fun to drive.

_____ My Jeep is tough and bold, but it is fun to drive too. It has a manual transmission, so I have better control of the engine when I take it into the mountains. Finally, riding high above the road makes driving more interesting.

_____ The colors also make it look rugged. It has black exterior paint and black leather seats. The Jeep logo is in bold white letters on the two side doors and on the steering wheel.

Your Own Writing

Planning Your Body Sentences

A. *Before you begin writing the body sentences for your paragraph, complete the outline.*

- Copy your topic sentence from page 36.

- List background information and descriptive details about your topic.

- Put the information and details in a logical sequence, such as time order or spatial order. You can always change the order later if you think of a better way.

Descriptive Paragraph

▶ Topic Sentence: _____

_____

▶ Background Information

1. _____

2. _____

3. _____

▶ Descriptive Details

1. _____

2. _____

3. _____

4. _____

5. _____

B. Checking in. *Discuss your outline with a partner. Tell your partner whether . . .*

- there is enough background information about the topic.

- you can imagine this business, product, or logo based on the descriptive details.

- anything is unclear.

Based on your partner's feedback, you may want to rewrite parts of your outline.

■ THE CONCLUDING SENTENCE(S)

In the final sentences of a descriptive paragraph, you wrap up or close the paragraph. There are many ways to do this. Sometimes writers restate or summarize the controlling idea in different words. In addition, they may use the transition words *in conclusion, in all, all in all, in summary,* or *in closing* to signal the ending. Other writers do not summarize or restate the controlling idea or use transition words at all. They signal the ending by giving a strong observation or a lasting impression about the topic.

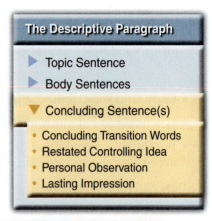

The Descriptive Paragraph

▶ Topic Sentence
▶ Body Sentences
▼ Concluding Sentence(s)
 • Concluding Transition Words
 • Restated Controlling Idea
 • Personal Observation
 • Lasting Impression

Examples:

All in all, I like Muji's products and appreciate the company's focus on simplicity. As a result of its no-branding policy, I think Muji has successfully created something out of nothing.

Hotel Vitale has succeeded in creating a powerful yet calming energy through its design. This hotel is more than just a place to stay; it is an unforgettable experience.

transition words   restated controlling idea   observation / impression

If you wanted to add a personal observation at the end of your paragraph, you could explain what you learned or feel about the person, place, or thing you described. If you want to express your final impression of the topic, you might present one or more key descriptive details about it.

Here are two strategies you might want to use to end your descriptive paragraph about a favorite business, product, or logo:

1. Explain why the business, product, or logo is unique and worth admiring.

2. Explain the impression the business, product, or logo has had on you and/or others.

Examples:

As a result of its no-brand policy, I think Muji has successfully made something out of nothing.

Hotel Vitale is more than just a place to stay; it is an unforgettable experience.

Focused Practice

Read the paragraph. Then answer the questions on page 43 about the concluding sentences.

A Symbol of Cars and Country

The Ferrari logo with a prancing horse is a strong and powerful image that appeals to many people all over the world. Ferrari is one of the most famous car manufacturers. It is an Italian company, and it makes very expensive sport cars. On the top of the Ferrari logo, there are three stripes in green, white, and red. Together the stripes represent the colors of the Italian flag. At the center of the logo is the famous Ferrari horse. It is a large black horse that is standing up high on its back two legs. The white outlines of its muscles make it look very powerful, just like the engines the company produces for its sports cars. The black color of the horse stands out against the yellow background of the logo. At the bottom of the logo is the Ferrari name in black letters. The letters are big and bold and show the strength of the Ferrari name for all to see. All in all, Ferrari has created a world-famous logo that reminds people of the powerful cars it produces. The logo is special because it speaks to the pride the company takes in being Italian; not many car companies pay respect to their home countries the way Ferrari does.

1. Underline the sentence that returns to the controlling idea of the topic sentence.

2. What strategy does the writer use to close the paragraph? _____

_____

Your Own Writing

Planning Your Conclusion

A. *How will you rephrase your controlling idea in a concluding sentence? List your ideas here.*

_____

_____

B. *What strategy will you use to close the paragraph?*

_____

_____

C. Checking in. *Share your ideas with a partner. Did your partner . . .*

- figure out an interesting way to return to his or her controlling idea?
- choose an effective concluding strategy?

Writing Your First Draft

Read the Tip for Writers. *Review your notes on pages 32, 36, and 41. Then write the first draft of your paragraph. When you are finished, give your paragraph a working title. Hand in your draft to your teacher.*

Review your notes on pages 32, 36, and 41.

Tip for Writers

When you write your first draft, check that you have used the conjunction *when* correctly to make the transitions between your ideas clear.

Revising your work is an essential part of the writing process. This is your opportunity to be sure that your paragraph has all the important pieces and that it is clear.

Focused Practice

A. *Read the descriptive paragraph.*

A Great Thai Restaurant

Paddy Thai was one of my favorite restaurants because of its cozy environment. The owners of Paddy Thai were originally from Thailand. When they moved to Houston, Texas, they decided to start a family-run restaurant that served traditional Thai dishes. The restaurant was successful, but it closed several years ago when the owners retired. Nonetheless, I still have fond memories of the place and my dining experiences there. The outside of the restaurant was striking in its simplicity. The building was small and white with a simple green sign. There was a wooden balcony for eating outside. When you walked inside, you felt as if you were entering the family's home. The walls were simply decorated. Pictures of famous Thai temples and photos of the owner's children and grandchildren hung in plain black frames on the walls. The dining room was long and narrow. It held 10 small tables. Some were round, and others were square or rectangular, so the interior felt very relaxed. There were no bright lights overhead, just a few romantic wall sconces. The tables were covered with rose tablecloths and lit candles, which always created a homey, intimate feeling. In all, I always enjoyed eating at Paddy Thai because of the delicious food, but I also loved how I felt in that place, as if I was eating in someone's own home. That is why I will always miss going there.

B. *Work with a partner. Answer the questions about the paragraph.*

1. What is the controlling idea of the paragraph? Underline the words that state it.

2. What background information has the writer included about the topic? Check (✓) any sentences that give background information.

3. What descriptive details does the paragraph present about the topic? Double underline any words or phrases that help you picture the topic.

4. What concluding transition words does the writer use toward the end of the paragraph? Circle them.

5. What strategy does the writer use to wrap up or close the description? _____

_____

C. Checking in. *Discuss your marked-up paragraphs with another pair of students. Then in your group, share one thing about the paragraph that you found the most interesting.*

Building Word Knowledge

The writer included different forms of the word *simple* in "A Great Thai Restaurant": *simplicity* (noun) and *simply* (adverb).

Work with a partner. Rewrite each sentence using the word in parentheses. If necessary, change the form of other words in the sentence too.

1. Apple's logo originally had many colors.

   (original – adj.) _Apple's original logo had many colors._

2. The new logo has a fresh look.

   (look – v.) _____

3. The silver logo shines.

   (shiny – adj.) _____

4. The iPad is an Apple product.

   (produce – v.) _____

Your Own Writing

Revising Your Draft

A. *Reread the first draft of your paragraph. Use the Revision Checklist to identify parts of your writing that might need improvement.*

B. *Review your plans and notes and your responses to the Revision Checklist. Then revise your first draft. Save your revised paragraph. You will look at it again in the next section.*

Revision Checklist

Did you . . .

☐ express your controlling idea in the topic sentence?

☐ give enough background information about your topic and arrange it logically?

☐ present and arrange descriptive details about your topic clearly?

☐ use prepositional phrases or the conjunction *when* to connect body sentences?

☐ restate your controlling idea in a new way in your concluding sentence(s)?

☐ use an effective concluding strategy?

☐ use word forms correctly?

☐ give your paragraph a good title?

■ GRAMMAR PRESENTATION

Before you hand in your revised paragraph, you must check it for any errors in grammar, punctuation, and spelling. In this section, you will learn about indefinite and definite articles. You will focus on this grammar when you edit and proofread your paragraph.

Articles: Indefinite and Definite

Grammar Notes	Examples

1. We can use **nouns** in two ways:
  a. A noun is **indefinite** when you and your reader do not have a specific person, place, or thing in mind.
  b. A noun is **definite** when you and your reader both <u>know or understand which person, place, or thing</u> you are talking about.
	• Romantic music makes customers spend more time at **a restaurant**.
	
	• **The restaurant** near our house serves excellent food.

2. To show that a noun is **indefinite,** use the **indefinite article *a/an*** or **no article**.
  a. Use the **indefinite article *a/an*** with <u>singular count nouns</u> that are **indefinite.**
 	
  b. Use **no article** with <u>plural count nouns</u> and with <u>non-count nouns</u> that are **indefinite**.
	singular count
	• ***A*** youth clothing **store** needs party music.
	       plural count plural count
	• There were **pictures** of famous **temples** in Thailand.
	       non-count
	• Upbeat **music** makes people happy.

3. Use the **definite article *the*** with most <u>common nouns</u> (count and non-count, singular and plural) that are **definite.**
 	
Use ***the*** when:
  a. a person, place, or thing is <u>unique</u>—there is only one
  b. the <u>context</u> makes it clear which person, place, or thing you mean
  c. the noun is mentioned for the <u>second time</u> (it is often indefinite the first time it is mentioned)
  d. a <u>phrase or an adjective</u> such as *first, best, right, most,* or *only* identifies the noun
  e. a <u>prepositional phrase</u> identifies the noun
	
	• It is one of the most recognized logos in ***the* world**.
	• When you walk into a youth clothing store, ***the* speakers** are in your face.
	• Muzak is ***a*** successful **company**. ***The* company** creates soundscapes for other businesses.
	
	• Trek makes ***the* best bicycles**.
	
	• When you employ ***the* science** <u>of Muzak</u>, workers tend to get more done.
	• Muzak is in ***the* business** <u>of selling emotion</u>.

Focused Practice

A. *Circle the correct article to complete the paragraph. Circle Ø if you don't need an article.*

Go Dyson

I really admire (1)(the)/ Ø products that the Dyson company makes because they are well made and friendly to (2) a(n) / the environment. (3) A(n) / The company was started in 1992 by (4) a(n) / the man named James Dyson. James Dyson's first product was (5) a(n) / Ø new kind of vacuum cleaner that did not use (6) the / Ø bags. He thought vacuums with bags lost (7) the / Ø power because they collected too much dust. (8) A(n) / The first Dyson vacuums came out in 1993. Today, they are sold all over (9) a(n) / the world, along with other successful Dyson products, including (10) the / Ø hand dryers and washing machines. Dyson products benefit from (11) a(n) / the use of newer forms of technology. They require less energy to use, and they make less waste. For example, (12) the / Ø hand dryers use air instead of paper towels, so they don't produce garbage. (13) The / Ø air pressure is so strong that hands dry in 12 seconds, so hand dryers use less electricity than other dryers. Dyson products are usually more expensive than other brands. However, when I consider how (14) the / Ø products work more cleanly and also tend to last longer, I think that Dyson products are well worth (15) a(n) / the extra money. I have owned my Dyson vacuum for over five years now, and I love it. It never loses power, and I know I am helping the environment because (16) a(n) / the only thing I have to throw away is dirt, not bags!

B. *Read and edit the paragraph. There are eleven errors in the use of the indefinite article. The first error has been corrected for you. Find and correct ten more by adding* a / an.

The Nike Swoosh

               a

I like the Nike logo because it has design that makes you think of movement and success. Nike is shoe company that is famous for making athletic sneakers. It has used the same logo for many years. The company calls the logo the Nike swoosh. The swoosh has feeling of movement. Swoosh is the sound that is made when person passes by very quickly. When people see the swoosh, they may think of marathon runner. The logo also suggests movement because it looks like wing. That is because the company is named after Nike, ancient Greek goddess who had

(continued)

---

wings and stood for victory. In addition, the logo suggests the image of checkmark. The checkmark suggests that Nike is good company that makes high-quality shoes. It may also represent how people feel when they finish race. In all, the Nike logo has unique meaning that I appreciate. When I see it, I hear it too.

C. *Read and edit the paragraph. Correct the capitalization if necessary. There are ten errors in the use of the definite article. The first error has been corrected for you. Find and correct nine more by adding* **the.**

iPad, iWant

The iPad is a popular and amazing device. It is a product from *the* Apple computer company. It has a large screen, Internet access, and many applications, such as a word processor. People can actually type on screen where a virtual keyboard shows up. Screen has a beautiful color and shine. It looks like a larger version of Apple iPhone screen, so it feels familiar. The iPad is easy to carry because it is just about size of a small book and weighs only one and half pounds. The iPad was an instant success in stores around world. One million iPads were sold in first month that device was available. Everyone seems to want iPad because it is easy to use, sleek, and innovative. Computers and phones have come a long way, and the iPad is just next chapter.

D. *Write five sentences related to the topic you chose on page 31. Use* indefinite *and* definite articles *or* no article. *These may be sentences you already have in your paragraph.*

1. _____

   _____

2. _____

   _____

3. _____

   _____

4. _____

   _____

5. _____

   _____

Your Own Writing

Editing Your Draft

A. *Use the Editing Checklist to edit and proofread your paragraph.*

B. *Prepare a clean copy of the final draft of your paragraph and hand it in to your teacher.*

Editing Checklist
Did you . . .
☐ include the definite and indefinite articles and use them correctly?
☐ use correct word forms, punctuation, and spelling?
☐ use prepositional phrases and the conjunction *when* correctly?

UNIT 3 Foods for Thought

IN THIS UNIT   You will be writing an opinion paragraph about a food.

Corn is a popular food in countries around the world, including the United States, China, and Brazil. Today, corn is a raw material in many foods because it is easy to produce and make into other products. For example, many processed foods use corn syrup instead of sugar as a sweetener. Corn is also used to make non-food products such as corn plastic, which is used in water bottles and shipping containers. It can also be made into ethanol, a kind of gasoline used in cars. What do you think about these many uses of corn? Do you think it is a good idea or a bad idea to use corn syrup, corn plastic, and corn gasoline?

Planning for Writing

■ BRAINSTORM

A. *Which of these items do you think contain corn? Check (✓) your answers. Then discuss them with a partner or as a class.*

_____ cereal   _____ shopping bags   _____ paper   _____ pet food

_____ drinking straws   _____ clothing   _____ ink   _____ crayons

B. *Read the information about corn. Which examples do you find surprising or interesting? Discuss those examples with a partner.*

Where Is Corn Today?

There are more uses for corn today than ever. Here are some examples:

- About 30 percent of corn grown in the United States is used to make ethanol.
- Many plastic water bottles are made from corn.
- Corn is the main ingredient in many types of dry pet food.
- Many soft drinks and cereals are sweetened with corn syrup.
- Corn is used in ink and paper for textbooks.

C. Using an Opinion Chart. When you express an opinion in writing, you can use a chart to record your opinion, reasons why you hold this opinion, and examples to support it.

Work with a partner. Reread the information about corn in Exercise B. Then use the opinion chart below to list an example that supports each reason.

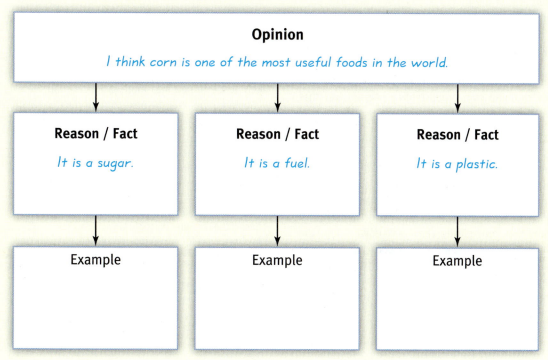

Opinion
I think corn is one of the most useful foods in the world.

Reason / Fact	Reason / Fact	Reason / Fact
It is a sugar.	*It is a fuel.*	*It is a plastic.*

Example	Example	Example

■ READ

Read the magazine article about the many uses of corn.

All About Corn

1   It is dinnertime. A mother serves her children fresh corn on the cob[1] with melted butter. The children take it for granted[2] that this is the only contact they've had with corn that day. In fact, corn fed the chickens that laid the eggs the children ate for breakfast. Corn syrup was the sweetener in the soda the children drank at lunchtime. Corn was even in the textbooks the children read at school! Cornstarch glued the pages of the books together. Corn was in the print's ink, and it was part of the sheets of paper, making them stronger and harder.

2   Though many people don't realize it, corn is one of the most influential crops in the world today. The cultivation[3] of corn (or maize) began between 6,000 and 7,000 years ago in parts of Mexico. Gradually, the cultivation of this plant spread across North and South America. Native people in the Americas used every part of the plant. They ate the corn kernels.[4] They turned the corn husks[5] into baskets and sleeping mats, and they used the corncobs to play special games. When the first Europeans came to the Americas, one of the gifts they received from Native Americans was corn.

3   Today, corn is grown all over the world, except in Antarctica. In the United States alone, approximately 13 billion bushels[6] of corn are grown each year. As in ancient times, corn is being used in a wide variety of ways—so many ways, it's hard to keep track of them. Clearly, corn is one of the most used foods today, but does it produce the most useful products? A look into three common corn products may help answer that question.

Plastic Plastic Everywhere

4   Once scientists figured out how to turn corn into an environmentally friendly type of plastic, corn plastic was used in all kinds of products from children's toys to packing materials. Unlike regular plastic (which is made from oil), corn plastic is biodegradable.[7] This means that corn plastic can break down under the right conditions. In this way, a corn plastic bottle would be a better choice than a regular plastic bottle. The only problem? Corn plastic doesn't biodegrade naturally, so people can't just throw it in the trash. It needs to go to special factories, which is hard to control.

Not Grass, but Corn

5   About half of all of the corn produced today is used as feed for cows, pigs, hens, and other farm animals. Before the 1960s, farm animals grazed on the land and ate grass. Today that's not the case. Farm animals live in smaller spaces and are fed corn, which is cheap to produce and fattens the animals more quickly. Although it is easier to produce more beef, eggs, and milk quickly and cheaply, there is a catch.[8] Raising animals in small spaces and feeding them corn can make the animals sick. Farmers give their animals antibiotics[9] to keep them from getting sick. These drugs become part of the meat, milk, and eggs we eat—which isn't good for us either. In addition, beef from corn-fed cows is fattier and less healthy than beef from grass-fed cows. For this reason, some people oppose the use of corn feed.

Corn in the Car

6   Today, corn is being used to make a cleaner burning fuel called ethanol. Traditional gasoline is made from oil. When cars burn gasoline, they produce carbon monoxide, a poisonous gas that can pollute the air. In contrast, ethanol is mostly oxygen, so it doesn't pollute the air. Critics say that to grow enough corn to produce ethanol harms natural resources in other ways: Land has to be cleared, and lots of water is wasted. Therefore, gassing the car or tractor with corn may not be the best way to go.

7   No matter what your point of view on the many uses of corn, you have to admit that this amazing plant is likely to be turned into more products than we ever imagined. What will the next corn product be? With a little imagination, the possibilities seem endless.

---

[1] **cob:** the hard part of corn that the yellow seeds grow on
[2] **take it for granted:** to believe that something is true without making sure
[3] **cultivation:** to prepare and use land for growing crops
[4] **kernels:** the small yellow pieces on a corn cob
[5] **husks:** the dry outer parts of corn
[6] **bushels:** units for measuring dry corn, equal to 8 gallons or 36.4 liters
[7] **biodegradable:** able to change naturally into substances that do not harm the environment
[8] **a catch:** a hidden problem or difficulty
[9] **antibiotics:** drugs that are used in order to kill bacteria and cure infections

Building Word Knowledge

Using Compound Nouns. In English, nouns are often combined with each other to form compounds. A compound noun is made up of two or more words—for example, *paper + clip = paperclip* and *desk + top = desktop*.

When you write, be sure to use compound nouns correctly. Some compound nouns are written as one word, as in *dinnertime* or *textbook*. Others are written as two words, as in *corn flakes* and *plastic bottle*. If you are not sure how to write a compound noun, check a dictionary. Look under each word in the compound. If the compound isn't listed, it's probably written as two words.

There are eight compound nouns with the word corn *in the reading on page 52. Two are listed below. Locate six more and add the words to the correct column in the chart. Then add any other compound nouns you know of with the word* corn. *Share your chart with a partner.*

One Word	Two Words
cornstarch	corn syrup

Focused Practice

A. *Based on the reading, match each controlling idea with the example that supports it.*

_____ **1.** Corn has a long history.

_____ **2.** Corn plastic can be better for the environment.

_____ **3.** Corn can make products less expensive.

_____ **4.** Corn can cause problems for farm animals.

_____ **5.** Corn can make cleaner burning fuel.

a. Unlike gasoline, ethanol doesn't produce carbon monoxide.

b. Humans have cultivated corn for 6,000 to 7,000 years.

c. Corn feed can make cows, pigs, and hens sick.

d. Corn-fed beef is cheaper than grass-fed beef.

e. Bottles with corn plastic break down more easily under the right conditions.

B. Read the **Tip for Writers.** *Which items did the writer explain? Which items did the writer assume that you, the reader, already knew? Check (✓) the correct items. Look back at the reading to check your answers.*

	Explained	Assumed
1. why corn is not grown in Antarctica	☐	☐
2. what *biodegradable* means	☐	☐
3. why corn is cheap to produce	☐	☐
4. why farmers feed animals corn	☐	☐
5. what carbon monoxide is	☐	☐

> ### Tip for Writers
>
> For any writing you do, it's important to identify your **audience**. Think about what your audience already knows. This helps you decide what kind of information to explain. Newspaper writers, for example, often write to a general audience, so in a science article, they may define scientific words that most people do not know.

C. *Look again at Exercise B. Think about the items that the writer chose to explain. Based on how the article is written, what audience do you think the writer had in mind? Check (✓) your answer. Then discuss your answer with a partner.*

_____ **a.** scientists

_____ **b.** farmers

_____ **c.** the general public

_____ **d.** businesspeople

D. *According to the article, corn is more than a food. It is used in a wide variety of products, including paper, fuel, and plastic. Which use of corn do you think is the most valuable? Why? Write a short paragraph and give your opinion. Try to use one or two compound nouns in your paragraph.*

_____

_____

_____

_____

_____

_____

_____

_____

_____

Writing an Opinion Paragraph

In this unit, you are going to write an opinion paragraph. When you write an opinion paragraph, you clearly state your views or beliefs about a topic and support these opinions with specific reasons and examples.

An opinion paragraph has the same parts as all paragraphs: a topic sentence, body sentences, and one or more concluding sentences.

The Opinion Paragraph
▶ Topic Sentence
▶ Body Sentences
▶ Concluding Sentence(s)

Step 1 Prewriting

For an opinion paragraph, the first prewriting step is to select a topic that you feel strongly about. The topic must be more than just a fact. For example, you can't write an opinion paragraph about what French fries are, but you can write one about why people should (or should not) eat them. After selecting a good topic, brainstorm reasons and examples to support your opinion.

Your Own Writing

Choosing Your Assignment

A. *Choose Assignment 1 or Assignment 2.*

   1. Think about a type of food that you believe is very useful. Explain why you think other people should value this food. Consider benefits that come from eating it or using other products made from it. Give at least two reasons to support your opinion.

   2. Think about a type of food that you believe is very bad for people or animals. Explain why it would be best to avoid eating and/or producing this food item. Give at least two reasons to support your opinion.

B. *Freewrite for 10 minutes on your topic. Here are some questions to get you started:*

   • What do you know or believe about this topic?

   • Why is the topic important to you?

   • What more might you need to find out in order to write an opinion paragraph about it?

C. Checking in. *Work with a partner who chose the same assignment. Discuss your topic and what you just wrote about it. Ask your partner some questions about his or her topic. For example, did your partner . . .*

- explain why he or she believes this food is useful or very bad for people or animals?
- describe the benefits or drawbacks of this food?
- express an opinion that can be supported with details?

Share your own opinion about your partner's food item. Based on your discussion, make changes or additions to your writing.

D. *Complete the opinion chart. Write your opinion. Then list reasons, facts, and examples to support it. Fill in as much information as you can. You will have a chance to review, change, or add information later in the unit.*

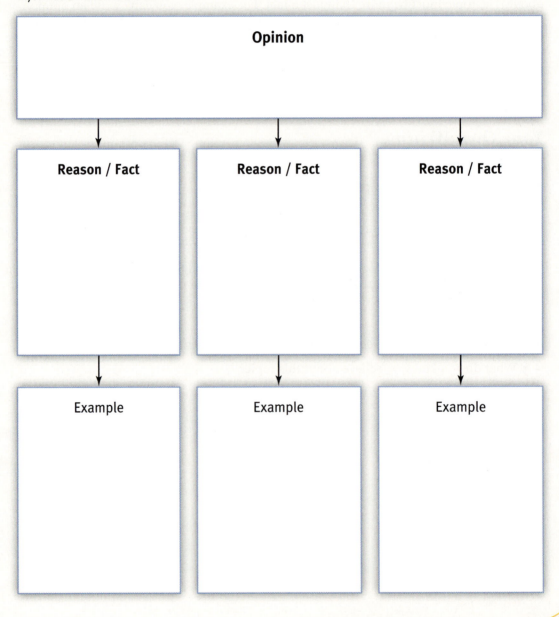

Opinion		
Reason / Fact	Reason / Fact	Reason / Fact
Example	Example	Example

■ THE TOPIC SENTENCE

In an opinion paragraph, the topic sentence presents the topic and your controlling idea (your personal view or belief) about the topic. Writers often let readers know that they are stating an opinion by using words such as *I believe, to me, I think,* or *in my opinion/view.* Writers also express their opinions by using the modal *should* and phrases such as *(one of) the best* or *the most.*

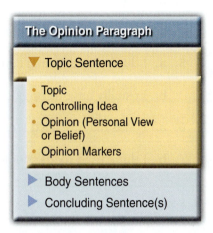

The Opinion Paragraph

▼ Topic Sentence
- Topic
- Controlling Idea
- Opinion (Personal View or Belief)
- Opinion Markers

▶ Body Sentences
▶ Concluding Sentence(s)

An opinion is different from a fact. A fact gives information that can be proven and measured. A fact is something that most people agree is true. The topic sentence of an opinion paragraph should not simply state a fact. Instead, it should express a personal view or belief you have about the topic—one that other people may agree or disagree with.

When you read the following topic sentences for an opinion paragraph, you can see the differences between a strong topic sentence and a weak one. The first two sentences clearly express a specific opinion about a food. The last two sentences state facts but do not express any opinion or use any opinion markers.

Examples:

          opinion marker   topic   opinion
Strong: Of all the foods in the world, I think that corn is the most useful.

  opinion marker   topic   opinion
Strong: I believe that more people should eat durian because this thorny fruit improves physical and mental health.

  opinion marker   topic   opinion
Strong: In my view, people throughout the world love rice for a good reason: It is one of the most useful food products.

  topic   fact, not opinion
Weak: Corn is a plant that can be turned into a kind of plastic, sugar, and gasoline.

  topic   fact, not opinion
Weak: Durian is a thorny fruit that comes from Southeast Asia.

         fact, not opinion   topic
Weak: Today scientists are able to make fuel from rice.

Focused Practice

A. *Circle the topic sentence that states an opinion (a personal view or belief).*

1. **a.** The avocado is considered a fruit because it has seeds.

   b. I think the avocado is one of the best fruits in the world.

2. **a.** There are many sugar substitutes that people can choose.

   b. I do not think there is anything wrong with using real sugar.

3. a. In my opinion, people should start their day with a bowl of oatmeal.

   b. Many people eat oatmeal in the morning because it keeps them full.

4. a. Chocolate has been eaten for thousands of years.

   b. A little chocolate should be part of a person's diet.

5. a. I think that drinking coffee is the best way to wake up.

   b. I usually have a cup of coffee with breakfast.

6. a. Foods that are fried tend to be high in both fat and cholesterol.

   b. I think fried foods should be avoided for a number of reasons.

B. *Read the topic sentences. Check (✓) the sentences that would make good topic sentences for an opinion paragraph. Discuss your answers with a partner.*

_____ **1.** People should drink water regularly for several reasons.

_____ **2.** I think people should avoid eating foods that have a lot of sugar.

_____ **3.** Eating breakfast gives people energy in the morning.

_____ **4.** In my opinion, restaurants should serve more vegetarian dishes.

_____ **5.** Many students skip meals because they are short on time.

_____ **6.** I believe that nuts are the best snack to choose when you are on the go.

C. *Read the topics. Write a topic sentence that expresses your opinion about each topic. Use opinion markers such as* I think, I believe, in my opinion, to me, should, *or* the most. *Discuss your answers with a partner.*

1. feeding corn to animals

   In my opinion, people should not feed corn to animals.

2. eating a big lunch

3. drinking soda

4. using corn plastic

5. eating canned vegetables

6. eating frozen foods

D. *Read the opinion paragraph and the sentences. Choose the best topic sentence for the paragraph. Then write it in the blank.*

Why We Should Eat Almonds

_____

_____

First of all, almonds are very good for you. For instance, most of their fat is what doctors consider "good" fat, which means it has important natural nutrients that keep the body healthy. Because they have a lot of protein, fiber, and vitamins, almonds are a much better snack to choose than chips or even crackers. Furthermore, almonds can be turned into other useful food products. For example, people can now buy almond butter and almond milk. Almond milk is excellent for people who cannot digest cow's milk. Almond milk is also lower in sugar than cow's milk, so it is healthier to drink. Finally, one of the most interesting benefits of almonds comes from the oil they produce. For instance, almond oil is a beneficial ingredient that is used in a number of beauty products today. Almond oil has vitamins that make dry skin moist, so it is found in many lotions and soaps. Several shampoos also contain almond oil because it makes hair stronger and healthier. All in all, it is hard to deny the many benefits that almonds provide. Almonds are a healthy snack choice, and they can also be turned into beneficial foods and beauty products. For these reasons, I think almonds are one of the most useful foods.

a. You might be surprised to learn that almonds are used in soaps, lotions, and shampoos.

b. More people should eat nuts because they are a healthy snack.

c. Many people do not know about the benefits of almonds and almond oil.

d. I think that almonds are one of nature's greatest gifts because they are both nutritious and useful.

Your Own Writing

Finding Out More

A. *Go online or visit the library to find out more about the food you selected. Look for additional reasons why your food is good or bad to eat or produce.*

- If you are searching online to find all of the health benefits of a food, such as almonds, you could key in the questions *Why are almonds healthy? Why are almonds useful?*

- Locate examples you can use to support your reasons and opinion.

- Check your opinion to be sure that it is supported by evidence, such as facts.

B. *Take notes on what you found out. Write about why your food item is useful, good, or bad for people or animals. Add new information to the opinion chart on page 56. Use this information when you write your paragraph. Be sure to note the sources for your information. (See the Appendix on pages 150–151.)*

C. Checking in. *Share your information with a partner. Did your partner . . .*

- find good, interesting reasons and examples to support his or her opinion?

- check his or her facts in at least three reliable sources?

Planning Your Topic Sentence

A. *Write a draft of your topic sentence. First list the topic, controlling idea, and any opinion markers that you can use to state your opinion. Remember: Your topic sentence should identify the food and your opinion about it. Look back at your freewriting and opinion chart to help you.*

Topic: _____

Controlling Idea about the Topic: _____

Opinion Marker(s): _____

Topic Sentence: _____

_____

B. Checking in. *Share your topic sentence with a partner. Did your partner . . .*

- clearly state the topic?

- show how he or she feels about the topic?

- include opinion markers?

Tell your partner what you expect to learn about his or her topic based on the topic sentence. Based on your partner's feedback, you may want to rewrite your topic sentence.

■ THE BODY SENTENCES

In the body sentences of an opinion paragraph, you develop and support your controlling idea, or opinion, by giving two or three reasons to support it. For each reason, you should also provide examples to show the reader why you think the way you do. To help readers understand each of your reasons and examples and how they are connected, you should use transition words.

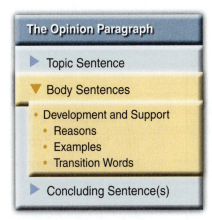

Giving Reasons and Examples

In an opinion paragraph, it is important to give reasons to explain your views and beliefs. For example, if you are writing about why almonds are a very useful food, you might give two reasons to support your opinion: (1) the food is nutritious, and (2) it is also used in beneficial skin products. When you write your opinion paragraph, you might introduce each reason with one of these listing-order transition words: *first, second, in addition, furthermore,* or *finally*.

After giving a reason, support it with examples and other supporting details. Good, vivid examples help readers better understand or picture an idea or situation more clearly and find your opinion more convincing. Suppose you are writing about the usefulness of corn products. You might ask yourself: *In what ways is ethanol beneficial? What kinds of products are made with corn plastic?* Then you could find the answers to these questions and use them to support your opinion.

Writers often give several example sentences to support each reason. To introduce an example, you can use the following example transition words: *for instance, for example, to illustrate, such as, specifically,* or *in particular*.

Example:

Topic Sentence: I think that almonds are one of nature's greatest gifts because they are both nutritious and useful.

Reason: First of all, almonds are very good for you.

Examples: *(In what way are they very good for you?)* For instance, most of their fat is what doctors consider "good" fat, which means it has important natural nutrients that keep the body healthier. Because they have a lot of protein, fiber, and vitamins, almonds are a much better snack to choose than chips or even crackers.

Reason: Furthermore, almonds can be turned into other useful products.

Examples: *(What kinds of products?)* For example, people can now buy almond butter and almond milk. Almond milk is excellent for people who cannot digest cow's milk. Almond milk is also lower in sugar than cow's milk, so it is healthier to drink.

Reason: Finally, one of the most interesting benefits of almonds comes from the oil they produce.

Examples: *(In what way is it beneficial?)* For instance, almond oil is a beneficial ingredient that is used in a number of beauty products today. Almond oil has vitamins that make dry skin moist, so it is found in lotions and soaps. *(What kinds of beauty products?)* Several shampoos also contain almond oil because it makes hair stronger and healthier.

listing-order transitions   example transitions

Foods for Thought **61**

Focused Practice

A. *Read the opinion paragraph. Then answer the questions.*

Don't Eat Fried French Fries!

Most people love the taste of French fries. However, they should avoid eating these fat-drenched potatoes because they are bad for your health. Why are fries bad for your health? First of all, they can cause high blood pressure. Your blood pressure measurement shows how easily your blood moves through your body, and it can be affected by how much salt you eat. Most French fries contain a lot of salt, so eating them increases your blood pressure. This, in turn, makes the heart work too hard. Because fries can cause high blood pressure, eating them can lead to heart disease. In addition, French fries are normally cooked in a type of oil that contains bad fats, called trans fats. These bad fats are also harmful to the heart. For example, they can clog the blood vessels that lead to the heart. The good news is that people don't need to eat regular French fries because there is a healthier option that tastes just as good. For instance, you can bake thinly sliced potatoes in the oven with some herbs and a little olive oil. The baked fries will still be tasty and crisp but will not have any trans fats or salt in them. It may be difficult to stop eating typical French fries, but when you do, you are helping your body, especially your heart.

---

1. Underline the topic sentence. How does the writer feel about eating French fries?

   _____

2. How many main reasons does the writer give to support the topic sentence?

   _____

3. What listing-order transition words does the writer use to introduce each reason? Circle them.

4. Look at the examples the writer includes. Then answer these questions:

   a. What transition words does the writer use to introduce each example? Circle them.

   b. What examples does the writer give to show the effects of French fries on your health?

   _____

   c. According to the writer, what is a healthier alternative to eating fried French fries?

   _____

B. *Read the opinion paragraph. Complete it by adding a second reason and examples as support. Discuss your completed paragraph with a partner.*

I think that coffee is the best drink to have in the morning. First of all, coffee makes early mornings a little more fun because there are so many kinds to choose from. For example, coffee drinkers can choose a bold dark roast or a lighter blend. They can also select from many different flavors, such as hazelnut or Irish cream. Because people have so many choices, they can make each morning different and a little more exciting when they're just waking up. Second of all, _____

_____

_____.

For these two reasons, I believe that people should start their mornings with a cup or two of delicious coffee.

Connecting with *So* and *Because*

In an opinion paragraph, writers often use the transition words *so* and *because* to show cause-effect relationships between their opinions, reasons, and examples. Writers can use *because* to introduce a reason and *so* to introduce a result or effect.

Examples:

Because they have a lot of protein, fiber, and vitamins, almonds are a much better snack choice than chips or even crackers.

Several shampoos also contain almond oil **because** it makes hair stronger and healthier.

Almond milk is also lower in sugar, **so** it is healthier.

Almond oil has vitamins that make dry skin moist, **so** it is found in many lotions and soaps.

| reason | result |

Focused Practice

A. *Complete the sentences with a reason or result. Discuss your answers with a partner.*

1. Because fries ___are high in salt___ , eating too many can be unhealthy. (*reason*)

2. People should avoid sweets because they _____. (*reason*)

3. Oranges have a lot of vitamin C, so they _____. (*result*)

4. Corn is cheap to produce, so it _____. (*result*)

5. Many people choose fast food because they _____. (*reason*)

B. *Combine the two sentences. Write one sentence with* **so** *and another with* because. *Discuss your answers with a partner.*

1. Corn can be easily turned into sugar. It is used in many foods.

   a. <u>Corn can be easily turned into sugar, so it is used in</u>

   <u>many foods.</u>

   b. <u>Because corn can be easily turned into sugar, it is used</u>

   <u>in many foods.</u>

> **Tip for Writers**
>
> When **because** is used at the beginning of a sentence, use a comma before the second clause. Do not use a comma when *because* is used between two clauses.

2. Coffee has a lot of caffeine. It is the perfect morning drink.

   a. _____

   b. _____

3. Canned foods must last a long time. They have many added chemicals.

   a. _____

   b. _____

4. Avocados are rich in vitamin E. They are good for your heart.

   a. _____

   b. _____

Your Own Writing

Planning Your Body Sentences

A. *Before you begin writing the body sentences for your paragraph, complete the outline.*

- Copy your topic sentence from page 60.
- List at least two main reasons for your opinion (personal view or belief).
- Brainstorm specific examples to help illustrate each of your reasons.
- Remember to ask and answer the questions *In what way(s)?* and *What kind(s)?* in order to think of good examples.

Opinion Paragraph

▶ Topic Sentence: _____

_____

  ▶ Reason: _____

    ▶ Examples: _____

    _____

▸ Reason: _____

  ▸ Examples: _____

  _____

▸ Reason: _____

  ▸ Examples: _____

  _____

B. Checking in. *Discuss your outline with a partner. Tell your partner . . .*

- whether the reasons clearly support your partner's opinion.

- whether the examples are convincing and explain *in what way(s)* and/or *what kind(s)*.

- which example you found the most interesting and why.

Based on your partner's feedback, you may want to rewrite parts of your outline.

■ THE CONCLUDING SENTENCE(S)

In an opinion paragraph, the concluding sentences are where you sum up your opinion and main reasons and offer final words of advice. To avoid repetition, you can use *synonyms*. A synonym is a word that has the same meaning or almost the same meaning as another word. *Dangers* and *risks* are synonyms. You can use synonyms to repeat something using different words.

Here are three strategies you might want to use to end your opinion paragraph about a food:

1. Return to your controlling idea and restate it in a new way, using synonyms to avoid repetition.

2. Sum up the main reasons you used to support your opinion.

3. Express a final thought or recommendation.

> **The Opinion Paragraph**
>
> ▸ Topic Sentence
> ▸ Body Sentences
> ▼ Concluding Sentence(s)
> - Restated Controlling Idea
> - Summary of Reasons
> - Final Thought or Recommendation

Examples:

Topic Sentence: I think that corn products shouldn't be used because they have hidden dangers.

Restated Topic Sentence: In conclusion, certain corn products carry risks, which is why I believe we should avoid using them.

Summary: Even though they seem like a good option, corn products can actually create more waste and demand more oil, both of which harm the environment.

Final Thought: No matter what your point of view on the many uses of corn, you have to admit that this amazing plant is likely to be turned into more products than we ever imagined.

Focused Practice

A. *Read the following topic sentences. For each one, write a concluding sentence that restates the topic and opinion in different words. Use synonyms to avoid repetition.*

1. People should drink water regularly for several reasons.

   In conclusion, I think that consuming eight glasses of water a day is a smart plan.

2. In my opinion, we should eat blueberries on a daily basis for two key health reasons.

   _____

3. I believe that nuts are the best snack to choose when you are on the go.

   _____

B. *Read the opinion paragraph and the sentences below it. Choose the concluding sentence that best summarizes the reasons the writer uses to support the controlling idea. Write the sentence in the blank.*

Take a Chocolate

I believe that a little chocolate should be a part of everyone's diet. First of all, chocolate actually has many health benefits. For instance, chocolate has chemicals called flavanoids that help protect the body's cells from damage. Flavanoids, which are found in the seeds of cacao plants, can also benefit the heart. Because chocolate has these properties, eating a small amount of this treat each day may actually help your body. In addition, people who are trying to lose weight or stay thin should eat chocolate regularly because it creates balance in their diet. For example, many dieters find it difficult to eat only healthy foods and avoid sweet ones. Dieters who don't let themselves eat sweets end up wanting them even more, so sometimes they overeat as a result. People who are watching their weight should have a small piece of chocolate each day. This would satisfy their need for something sweet without causing them to overeat. In conclusion, I think more people should consider eating a small amount of chocolate regularly. _____

_____

_____

---

a. However, I do not think that people should eat sweets because they cause weight gain.

b. Chocolate gets a bad name because it is sugary, and people don't know it can be healthy.

c. Chocolate is as good for you as it tastes, and it helps you maintain a balanced diet.

Your Own Writing

Planning Your Conclusion

A. *How will you rephrase your controlling idea in a concluding sentence? List your ideas here. Include any synonyms that come to mind.*

_____

_____

B. *What strategy will you use to close the paragraph?*

_____

C. **Checking in.** *Share your ideas with a partner. Did your partner . . .*

- use appropriate synonyms to use to rephrase the controlling idea?
- choose an effective conclusion strategy?

Writing Your First Draft

Read the **Tip for Writers.** *Review your notes on pages 56, 60, and 64–65. Then write the first draft of your paragraph. When you are finished, give your paragraph a working title. Hand in your draft to your teacher.*

> **Tip for Writers**
>
> When you write your first draft, be sure to explain important information for your audience (your classmates and teacher).

Step 3   Revising

Revising your work is an essential part of the writing process. This is your opportunity to be sure that your paragraph has all the important pieces and that it is clear.

Focused Practice

A. *Read the opinion paragraph.*

Delightful Durian

I believe that more people should eat durian because this thorny fruit from Southeast Asia improves both physical and mental health. First of all, durian helps to keep your body in healthy condition because it is high in vitamins and minerals. For example, it has a lot of iron, which is good for the brain, the muscles, and the immune system. In addition, durian is believed to be a natural healer. For instance, in some parts of Asia where durian grows naturally, doctors use the fruit to cleanse

(continued)

---

the blood and to reduce fevers. The fruit has chemicals that can prevent blood clots. The chemicals can also reduce inflammation in the body, so eating durian might stop or prevent headaches. Finally, durian is known to have positive effects on a person's mood. Specifically, it may be able to make people happier because it contains a chemical called tryptophan. Tryptophan can reduce feelings of anxiety and depression. Getting tryptophan from durian fruit can lift a person's mood, so it is good for people who suffer from stress. In all, durian is not a well-known fruit, but I think more people should try it. Health food, healer, and stress reliever—this miracle food has many benefits for both the body and the mind.

B. *Work with a partner. Answer the questions about the paragraph.*

1. What is the controlling idea (the point of view or opinion) of the paragraph? Underline it.

2. What three reasons does the paragraph include in support of the controlling idea? Underline the sentences that introduce them.

3. What examples support and develop the main reasons? Check (✓) the sentences that provide specific examples.

4. Where does the writer restate the controlling idea and summarize the reasons in a single sentence? Circle it.

5. Which sentences use *because* to introduce reasons? Underline the sentences.

6. Which sentences use *so* to introduce results or effects? Underline the sentences.

C. Checking in. *Discuss your marked-up paragraphs with another pair of students. Then in your group, share one thing about the paragraph that you found the most interesting.*

Building Word Knowledge

The writer included many compound nouns in "Delightful Durian," including *immune system*, *blood clots*, *headaches*, and *miracle food*.

Work with a partner. Add a word from the box to each word below to form a compound noun. Use a dictionary to decide whether the compound should be written as one word or two. Then write a sentence of your own for each pair of compounds. The first one is done for you.

ache	blood	food	relief	~~system~~

1. nervous _____*system*_____   digestive _____*system*_____

The nervous system controls movement, and the digestive system absorbs

vitamins and minerals from food.

2. _____ bank   _____ type

_____

_____

3. tooth _____   stomach _____

_____

_____

4. junk _____   comfort _____

_____

_____

5. pain _____   cold _____

_____

_____

Your Own Writing

Revising Your Draft

A. *Reread the first draft of your paragraph. Use the Revision Checklist to identify parts of your paragraph that might need improvement.*

B. *Review your plans and notes and your responses to the Revision Checklist. Then revise your first draft. Save your revised paragraph. You will look at it again in the next section.*

Revision Checklist

Did you . . .

☐ present your topic and point of view in the topic sentence?

☐ use opinion markers to emphasize your point of view?

☐ explain any terms or information that your audience might not know?

☐ present two or three main reasons to support your opinion?

☐ provide specific examples to illustrate each of your reasons?

☐ introduce your reasons and examples with transition words?

☐ restate your topic sentence and summarize your reasons in your concluding sentence(s)?

☐ use an effective concluding strategy?

☐ use *so* and *because* correctly?

☐ use any compound nouns in your paragraph?

☐ give your paragraph a good title?

■ GRAMMAR PRESENTATION

Before you hand in your revised paragraph, you must check it for any errors in grammar, punctuation, and spelling. In this section, you will learn about the modals *can* and *should*. You will focus on this grammar when you edit and proofread your essay.

Can and *Should*

Grammar Notes	Examples

1. *Can* and *should* are modals. Like all modals,
  • they are followed by the <u>base form</u> of a verb.
  modal + base form of verb
  • they have the same form for all subjects. (They do not use *-s* for the third-person singular.)
  • they form the negative with *not*. (They do not use *do*.)
	• Fried foods **can cause** high blood pressure.
	
	• A little chocolate **can be** healthy.
	  Not: It ~~cans~~ be healthy.
	
	• Some people **cannot digest** cow's milk.
	  Not: They ~~doesn't can~~ digest it.

2. Use ***should*** to say that something is advisable (a good idea). Use ***should not*** to say that something is not advisable (a bad idea).	• More people **should try** durian. • People **should not eat** French fries.
3. Use ***can*** or ***cannot*** to show present and future ability.	• Corn **can become** fuel. • People **can make** baked fries.

Note: When writing, avoid using the contracted forms *can't* and *shouldn't*.

Focused Practice

A. *Read and edit each sentence. Look for errors with* can *and* should. *If there is an error, correct it. The first one is done for you.*

> *should*
1. Nuts ~~can to~~ last a long time without going bad.

2. I do not can understand why people drink so much coffee.

3. Parents should not let young children eat fast food.

4. It can takes less time for corn plastic to biodegrade.

5. There should be more healthy food options in school cafeterias.

6. More companies should to use products made of corn plastic.

7. You can finding many foods with corn syrup at the grocery store.

8. I should not to eat chocolate, but I cannot help myself.

B. *Complete the sentences with the verbs in parentheses. Use* should *or* should not.

1. Car manufacturers _____ cars that use only ethanol.
   (make)

2. People _____ greasy foods because they are high in
   (eat)
   cholesterol.

3. School cafeterias _____ French fries because children need
   (serve)
   to eat healthy foods.

4. People _____ water regularly because it keeps the body
   (drink)
   hydrated.

5. According to doctors, people _____ five servings of fruits
   (consume)
   and vegetables per day.

6. Parents _____ their children eat too many sugary foods.
   (let)

7. You _____ eating a big meal before going to bed because it
   (avoid)
   can make you gain weight.

8. People _____ the benefits of durian until they have tried it.
   (doubt)

C. *Complete the paragraph with the verbs in parentheses. Use* can *or* cannot.

In my view, people throughout the world love rice for a good reason: It is

one of the most useful food products. Rice _____*can go*_____ with many
                                              1. (go)

dishes. For instance, people _____ it with both vegetable and
                                  2. (use)

meat dishes, and it is often eaten daily in Asian countries such as China and Japan.

People _____ with other products made from rice too. Rice that
          3. (cook)

is ground _____ rice flour, which is used for baking. People
             4. (become)

_____ rice noodles in many Asian restaurants and supermarkets
   5. (find)

as well. In addition, people _____ rice into fuel. For example, the
                                 6. (turn)

Japanese have developed a rice-based gasoline. It _____ added
                                                       7. (be)

to gasoline for some cars. Many cars _____ rice-based gasoline
                                          8. (use)

yet because they don't have the right technology, but rice fuel might become a

reality in the future. In conclusion, people _____ the usefulness
                                                  9. (deny)

of rice. It is a staple food in many parts of the world, and one day, it might even

power your car!

D. *Write five sentences related to the topic you chose on page 55. Use* can(not) *and* should (not). *These may be sentences you already have in your paragraph.*

1. _____

_____

2. _____

_____

3. _____

_____

4. _____

_____

5. _____

_____

Your Own Writing

Editing Your Draft

A. *Use the Editing Checklist to edit and proofread your paragraph.*

B. *Prepare a clean copy of the final draft of your paragraph and hand it in to your teacher.*

Editing Checklist
Did you . . .
☐ include *can* and *should* and use them correctly?
☐ use correct verb forms, punctuation, and spelling?
☐ use compound nouns and other words correctly?

4 Public Spaces

IN THIS UNIT You will be writing a persuasive essay about a place you know.

Amman is the capital of Jordan. It is a city with a blend of old and new. Tall skyscrapers are found in neighborhoods that are thousands of years old. Architects and city officials are trying to make Amman a more "livable" city. Now the people of Amman are trying to decide whether the changes that have been made are an improvement or not. How do you think cities can become more livable?

Planning for Writing

■ BRAINSTORM

A. *Think about what you like about cities. Rank the features from 1 (most favorite) to 6 (least favorite). Then discuss your answers with a partner.*

_____ **a.** public parks

_____ **b.** expensive clothing stores

_____ **c.** outdoor markets

_____ **d.** international restaurants

_____ **e.** public libraries

_____ **f.** museums

B. Using a T-chart. When you are writing a persuasive essay on an issue, you can use a graphic organizer, such as a T-chart, to record your views and beliefs as well as the opposing ones.

Look at the types of changes that have taken place recently in Amman, Jordan. Decide whether you are **for** *or* **against** *each change. Then add the changes to the appropriate column on the T-chart. Discuss your answers with a partner.*

tall skyscrapers	sidewalks on city streets	streetlamps at night
fast-food restaurants	fancy restaurants downtown	benches along sidewalks

Amman's New Changes	
For	**Against**

■ READ

Read the travel blog about one traveler's view of Amman, Jordan.

A Walk through Past and Present Amman

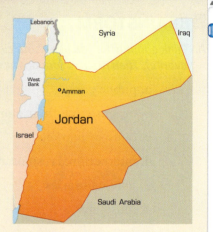

1   **March 5**—I'm a travel writer in search of fascinating places. I have just arrived in Amman, Jordan, and this capital city is one such place. It's springtime here. Although the city is over 10,000 years old, the air smells as fresh as a newly planted garden.

2   Over 2 million people now call Amman home. Many live in East Amman, the older part of the capital. Daily life at one of the famous street markets, called souqs, is full of color. As I stroll through a souq, I spot a beautiful necklace, with beads as red as ripe cherries. I hear locals shouting as they bargain for brightly colored woven baskets and handmade dresses. I pass a vendor who is selling perfumes made from jasmine and other sweet-scented flowers. When the sunlight touches the blue, green, and red glass of the perfume bottles, they look as colorful as a stained glass window.

3   West Amman is very different—it's the center of business. The architecture is more modern. Take, for example, the Jordan Gate Towers. These glass skyscrapers stand there like two giant mirrors, reflecting the surrounding buildings and high hills in the distance. In West Amman, the fancy restaurants and expensive clothing stores are very different from the traditional souqs of East Amman. East and West Amman almost feel like two different cities.

4   However, I have heard that Amman has undergone a big change recently—a new plan is changing the look and feel of the city and bringing the two parts closer together. I meet a man who tells me the city has a new slogan: "A livable city is an organized city, with a soul." I wonder, what gives the new Amman a soul? And how do the people who live here feel about their changing city?

5   **March 9**—Wakalat Street, East Amman. An older gentleman tells me that Wakalat Street used to be congested[1] with automobiles and commercial signs. "It was ugly and industrial with no heart," he says. The city's master plan has changed all that. Wakalat is Amman's first pedestrian-only street,

so there are no cars. Trees and sidewalks have replaced the streets. People walk and window-shop, drink coffee in a local café, and push baby strollers in peace. It's friendly and inviting.

6   But not everyone is happy about the changes. Some local shop owners complain about losing money. Before, only the wealthy shopped here—they drove in, parked in the store parking lots, spent their money, and drove away. Businesses did well.

7   Now rich and poor and many young people walk the sidewalks of Wakalat. One local shopkeeper complains that the young people are "like a pack of angry dogs." He says they have scared his customers away. To keep the business owners happy, the city has removed most of the benches. But the people still come—including me.

---

[1] **congested:** too full or blocked because of too many vehicles or people

76   UNIT 4

8　　**March 12**—Rainbow Street, West Amman. I walk along a sidewalk lined with benches, a sign of the new plan. These new, flat sidewalks are not just for convenience. They represent the city's desire to bring rich and poor together—face-to-face—through design. Locals feel comfortable here, and so do I.

9　　Seventeen-year-old Samar al-Sarayreh sits with her sister overlooking the city. "When I come here now," she says, "there are fewer cars and there is a place to sit down and relax outside the house. It's a public place for everyone."

10　　Even when cars pass through, they can't drive fast anymore. Architect Rami F. Daher replaced the paved streets with cobblestones[2] in order to force cars to slow down. Smooth as ice under my feet, the stones give the street an old, weathered[3] look.

11　　**March 15**—Amman has undergone[4] a radical change. This ancient city has turned into a vibrant[5] gathering place. As I walk these streets for the last time, I can see and feel the transition the city is experiencing. What a difference benches and sidewalks can make to a city and its people. To some, they cause problems; to others, they give the city a soul.

---

[2] **cobblestones:** small round stones set in the ground, especially in the past, to make a hard surface for a road
[3] **weathered:** gradually changed in appearance by the wind, rain, and sun
[4] **undergone:** experienced
[5] **vibrant:** exciting, full of energy, and interesting

Building Word Knowledge

Using Similes. Writers often make imaginative comparisons to help readers experience a person, place, or thing in a unique way. When a writer uses the word *like* or *as* in an imaginative comparison, it is called a *simile*. For example, in "A Walk through Past and Present Amman," the writer compares two glass skyscrapers to giant mirrors. An effective simile invents a new way of looking at or experiencing something.

Complete the similes from the reading on page 76. Then discuss with a partner why you think the writer used each simile.

1. The air smells as fresh as _____.

2. I spot a beautiful necklace with beads as red as _____.

3. When the sunlight touches the blue, green, and red glass of the perfume bottles, they

   look as colorful as _____.

4. One local shopkeeper complains that the young people are like _____

   _____.

5. Smooth as _____ under my feet, the stones give the street an old,

   weathered look.

Focused Practice

A. *Work with a partner. How has the writer described different places in Amman? Match each description to the correct place.*

_____ **1.** Amman, Jordan   **a.** There are fancy restaurants and clothing stores.

_____ **2.** East Amman   **b.** Two million people call it home.

_____ **3.** West Amman   **c.** Its famous souqs are loud and colorful.

_____ **4.** Wakalat Street   **d.** The streets are paved with cobblestones to slow traffic.

_____ **5.** Rainbow Street   **e.** It is Amman's first pedestrian-only street.

B. *Read the* Tip for Writers *and the examples of descriptive details below.*

Examples:

The warm, yeasty fragrance of freshly baked bread filled the air.

Bright-blue flowers with white centers grew in lacy vines along the wall.

Now reread paragraph 2 of the reading on page 76. Answer the questions by giving descriptive details from the reading.

> ### Tip for Writers
>
> When you write about a place, use **descriptive details** that appeal to the senses to help readers imagine how something smells, tastes, or looks.

1. What do the baskets look like? _____

2. What do the perfumes smell like? _____

3. What colors are the perfume bottles? _____

C. *Match the people in the article with their opinions about the new changes in Amman. Look back at the reading to check your answers.*

_____ **1.** the travel writer   **a.** Benches invite too many young people.

_____ **2.** a local shopkeeper   **b.** There is a place to sit down and relax outside.

_____ **3.** Samar al-Sarayreh   **c.** This ancient city is a vibrant gathering place.

D. *After reading "A Walk through Past and Present Amman," do you think old cities like Amman should have tall, modern skyscrapers? Why or why not? Write a short paragraph explaining your views and beliefs on the topic. Use descriptive details to support your opinion.*

_____

_____

_____

_____

_____

_____

_____

_____

Writing a Persuasive Essay

You are going to write a persuasive essay that tries to convince people to share your point of view about a place. You will use descriptive details, similes, and other supporting information to convince readers to understand and maybe even agree with your argument or reasoning.

Like an opinion paragraph, a persuasive essay contains three parts.

An essay is a group of paragraphs about one topic. It is similar to a paragraph in many ways, except that it is longer and more developed. An essay usually has an introductory paragraph, one or more body paragraphs, and a concluding paragraph.

Paragraphs and essays have the same basic structure, as shown in the diagram.

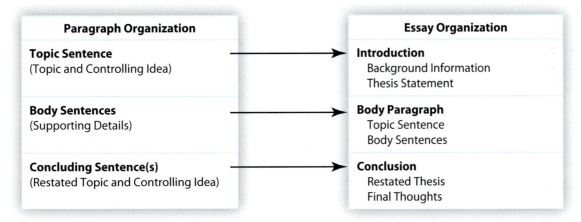

Paragraph Organization	Essay Organization
Topic Sentence (Topic and Controlling Idea)	**Introduction** Background Information / Thesis Statement
Body Sentences (Supporting Details)	**Body Paragraph** Topic Sentence / Body Sentences
Concluding Sentence(s) (Restated Topic and Controlling Idea)	**Conclusion** Restated Thesis / Final Thoughts

Note the similarities between single paragraphs and essays.

- The *thesis statement* in an essay is like the *topic sentence* in a paragraph. The thesis gives the topic and controlling idea of the whole essay.

- The *body paragraphs* are the middle paragraphs of an essay. They divide the supporting ideas into separate paragraphs. Like a single paragraph, a body paragraph usually begins with a *topic sentence* that states the controlling idea, or focus, of the paragraph. Both a single paragraph and a body paragraph within an essay contain supporting details, or evidence, to explain the topic sentence.

- The *conclusion* in an essay is like the *concluding sentence(s)* in a paragraph. It includes a restatement of the essay's controlling idea and a few closing statements.

When writing a persuasive essay, the first step is to select a topic that people have differing opinions about. Next, analyze your own feelings and opinions about the topic. As you decide on your own view or belief, be sure to consider the opposite point of view as well: Why might people disagree with your argument?

Your Own Writing

Choosing Your Assignment

A. *Choose Assignment 1 or Assignment 2.*

    1. Think about a place—such as a park, city center, or neighborhood—that could be changed or improved in some way. Decide whether you think it is worth the time and money to change this place. Take a position for or against some type of change and support your decision. Use opinion markers to present your argument.

    2. Imagine that your school has recently bought more land to build on. Some students want the school to build a new athletic facility. Other students want to turn the land into a small park with a garden, benches, and tables. Choose one side and support your decision. Use opinion markers to present your argument.

B. *Freewrite for 10 minutes on your assignment. Here are some questions to get you started:*

- What do you know or believe about this place?

- What is the place like now and what would it be like with the change(s)?

- Which types of change do you support?

- Which types do you oppose? Why?

- Why might some people disagree with your argument or point of view?

C. **Checking in.** *Work with a partner who chose the same assignment. Discuss your topic and what you just wrote about it. Ask your partner some questions about his or her topic. For example, did your partner . . .*

- describe what the place is like and how it might be better or worse because of the change(s)?

- explain why he or she supports or opposes certain kinds of change?

- consider other people's points of view on the issue?

- use expressive words to present his or her argument?

Share your point of view on your partner's topic. Based on your discussion, make changes or additions to your writing.

D. *Complete the T-chart. Write the arguments or reasoning you can use* **for** *your point of view on the issue. Also, write the arguments others might use* **against** *your point of view. Fill in as much information as you can. You will have a chance to review, change, or add information later in the unit.*

Topic: _____	
For	**Against**

■ THE INTRODUCTION

The introductory paragraph in an essay contains two parts:

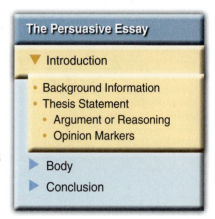

1. **Background information** about the topic of the essay to help your reader to understand and become interested in the topic. To think of background information, ask yourself, *What does the reader need to know about the topic? What information do I need to provide?* Do not give too many details. You will develop your topic further in the body of the essay.

2. A **thesis statement** that presents the controlling idea of the whole essay; it may be one sentence or two. Just as the topic sentence in a paragraph introduces what the paragraph will be about, the thesis statement presents the controlling idea that the writer will support in the rest of the essay.

In a persuasive essay, the background information often presents various, sometimes opposing, views people have about the issue. Then the thesis statement presents the writer's argument or reasoning about the issue. The thesis statement in a persuasive essay is similar to the topic sentence in an opinion paragraph. It often includes opinion markers (such as *I think, I believe, in my opinion, I strongly support/oppose*) to show that the writer's argument is based on an opinion.

Examples:

opinion marker and argument   topic
In my opinion, there are some problems with Amman's new plan.

opinion marker   topic   argument
I believe that Amman's new plan has made the city a better place to live.

Focused Practice

A. *Read the following essay assignment and the sentences. Check (✓) the details that you might use as background information for an introductory paragraph on this topic. Discuss your answers with a partner.*

> *Some people like Amman's new master plan, but others think it has problems. Is the new plan a good or bad change for the city?*

_____ **1.** Amman, the capital of Jordan, is over 10,000 years old.

_____ **2.** Falafel on pita bread is a typical kind of street food found in Amman.

_____ **3.** A *souq* is an outdoor market where people can buy food and clothing.

_____ **4.** Amman is a city with a soul.

_____ **5.** Today, Amman is growing rapidly.

_____ **6.** In the past, there weren't many outdoor spaces for the public to enjoy.

_____ **7.** The Jordan Gate Towers are modern skyscrapers located in the sixth circle.

_____ 8. Now there are more benches and sidewalks so that people can enjoy the souqs and sights in East Amman and more skyscrapers and fancy restaurants to visit in West Amman.

_____ 9. Recently, Amman has developed a new plan to change the city.

_____ 10. Some people believe that these changes make the city more livable, but others think they cause too many problems.

B. *Read the following essay assignment and the sentences. Then check (✔) the sentences that would make a good thesis statement for an essay on this topic. Discuss your answers with a partner.*

> ### Describe a place that you like very much and explain why readers should visit it.

_____ 1. Tokyo is a nice place to live because there are many things to do, but it is also very expensive.

_____ 2. My hometown is a beautiful place.

_____ 3. Tourists would enjoy visiting Boston, Massachusetts; it has beautiful architecture and excellent shopping.

_____ 4. You should travel to Istanbul at least once in your life.

_____ 5. If you visit Saigon, Vietnam, you will never forget it; Saigon has amazing markets for shoppers and good, cheap restaurants.

_____ 6. I prefer to visit small towns; they are more peaceful than cities, and the people are usually friendlier.

_____ 7. Going to Paris is like looking at a wonderful painting. Make Paris your next travel destination so that you can experience its unforgettable places and people.

C. *Read the model introductory paragraph for the following essay assignment. Then discuss the questions with a partner.*

> ### Some people like Amman's new master plan, but others think it has problems. Is the new plan a good or bad change for the city?

Amman, the capital of Jordan, is over 10,000 years old. Today, the city is growing rapidly. Recently, Amman has developed a new plan to change the city. In the past, there weren't many outdoor spaces for the public. Now there are more benches and sidewalks so that people can enjoy the souqs and sights in East Amman and more skyscrapers and fancy restaurants to visit in West Amman. Some Ammanis believe that these changes make the city more livable, but others think they have caused problems. I think that Amman's new plan has benefited the city in two key ways. It has made the city a friendlier place, and it has encouraged diversity.

1. Which details from Exercise A did the writer include as background?

2. Why do you think the writer used some details but not others?

3. Underline the thesis statement. What kind of information do you think the essay will present to support the writer's argument, or reasoning?

Your Own Writing

Finding Out More

A. *Learn more about the topic you chose on page 80.*

- If you chose Assignment 1, go online or to the library to find out more about the place you selected. Find out how people feel about the place by reading articles and editorials on online blogs or in the newspaper. Use keywords when you search for information online, for example: [*name of place*] + *public opinion*, *problems*, or *changes*. You may also want to talk to people who know about the place to see how they feel about the proposed change.

- If you chose Assignment 2, research what outdoor or athletic spaces your school currently offers. Go online or to the library to find out about similar situations in other schools. Visit your school's website or talk to people who work at the school. Interview students in your classes. Describe the two options to them and ask them how they feel about each one.

B. *Take notes on what you found out. (See the Appendix on pages 150–151 for noting key information about any sources you use.) Add new arguments for or against your topic to your T-chart on page 81. Use this information when you write your essay.*

C. **Checking in.** *Share your information with your partner. Did your partner . . .*

- gather enough background about the place and the proposed changes to it?

- find reasons why people would be for or against the change(s)?

- use at least three reliable sources?

Planning Your Introduction

A. *List the background information you will need to include in your introduction.*

_____

_____

_____

B. *Write a draft of your thesis statement. Make sure your thesis statement clearly presents your argument and supporting reasons. Look back at your freewriting and T-chart to help you.*

_____

_____

➡

- clearly present an argument for or against the proposed change(s)?

- include opinion markers and other words to make the argument clear and convincing?

Tell your partner what you like about his or her thesis statement. Based on your partner's feedback, you may want to rewrite your thesis statement.

■ THE BODY

The body paragraphs make up the "middle" part of an essay. Just as a paragraph contains a group of sentences that support the topic sentence, an essay contains one or more paragraphs that present information in support of the thesis statement.

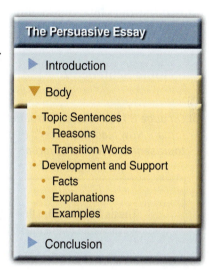

The Persuasive Essay

▶ Introduction

▼ Body
- Topic Sentences
  - Reasons
  - Transition Words
- Development and Support
  - Facts
  - Explanations
  - Examples

▶ Conclusion

Writing Topic Sentences

In an essay, each body paragraph usually begins with a topic sentence. These sentences often rephrase and build on some information from the thesis statement. In a persuasive essay, each topic sentence can present a specific reason why the writer holds a particular opinion (view or belief). Then the rest of the body paragraph develops and supports that reason with details, such as facts, examples, and explanations.

When writing a four-paragraph essay about a proposed change to a place, your topic sentences might focus on two of the main reasons you are for or against the change. To introduce a reason or controlling idea, you can use transition words. For example, you might use the listing-order transitions that you learned about in Unit 3: *first, second, in addition,* or *finally.*

Example:

Thesis Statement: Tourists would enjoy visiting Boston, Massachusetts; it has beautiful architecture and excellent shopping.

Topic Sentence 1: First of all, visitors to Boston can see historic houses and churches as well as modern skyscrapers.

Topic Sentence 2: In addition, Boston offers many interesting shops and small boutiques where tourists can find unique objects and clothes.

You can also use transition words that show the order of importance of your reasons or ideas; for example, your topic sentences might include words such as *main, key, primary, most important, also important,* or *of equal importance.*

Example:

Thesis Statement: I strongly support the recent changes in Amman. They have helped to unify the city, and they have encouraged a wide range of lifestyles.

Topic Sentence 1: The main reason why I support the changes in Amman is that they have brought different parts of the city together.

Topic Sentence 2: The changes also show off the city's diversity, which is another key reason why I believe they are positive.

Focused Practice

A. *Read the following thesis statements. Write two topic sentences for each one. Identify a specific reason (an advantage or disadvantage) and include a transition word (listing order or order of importance). You can scan "A Walk through Past and Present Amman" on pages 76–77 for ideas.*

1. **Thesis Statement:** I support Amman's new plan for two reasons. It has increased safety and encouraged a stronger sense of community.

   Topic Sentence 1: *First, it has made the streets safer to walk on.*

   Topic Sentence 2: _____

2. **Thesis Statement:** In my opinion, Amman's new plan has two major disadvantages. It has hurt businesses and encouraged wild behavior among some young people.

   Topic Sentence 1: _____

   Topic Sentence 2: _____

B. *On page 83 you read an introductory paragraph for a persuasive essay about changes in Amman, Jordan. Now read the writer's thesis statement again and the first body paragraph. Then write a topic sentence for the paragraph.*

Thesis Statement: I think that Amman's new plan has benefited the city in two key ways. It has made the city a friendlier place, and it has encouraged diversity.

_____

_____

_____

Historically, Amman has been divided into two parts. West Amman is the wealthier section that is the city's center of business. East Amman is older, more traditional, and less wealthy. They used to be like two different worlds. However, the new plan has brought the rich and poor together in common spaces. On Rainbow and Wakalat Streets, Ammanis and visitors can walk on sidewalks or sit on benches. Because of the benches, people from different backgrounds are more likely to interact with each other face-to-face. I think this makes people in the city feel closer to one another, even to strangers. For example, when someone sits down next to another person, the two often start a conversation. On sidewalks, people say hello and smile at those they pass by. Without public spaces like these, it would be harder to develop a feeling of community in Amman.

Developing a Body Paragraph

In Unit 3, you learned the importance of supporting an opinion with reasons and examples. The same is true of an essay. The topic sentence of each body paragraph must be developed and supported with details, or evidence: facts, explanations, and examples.

Example:

Fact: On Rainbow and Wakalat Streets, people can walk on sidewalks or sit on benches.

Explanation: Because of the benches, people from different backgrounds are more likely to interact with each other face-to-face.

Example: For example, when someone sits down next to another person, the two often start a conversation.

Some writers return to the controlling idea and sum up the reason at the end of each body paragraph. Others wait until the concluding paragraph to sum up their reasoning and argument.

Example:

Summary: Without public spaces like these, it would be harder to develop a feeling of community in Amman.

No Summary: At busy hours, such as lunchtime and evenings, the crowds come at you like an overpowering wave. It is hard not to run into other people.

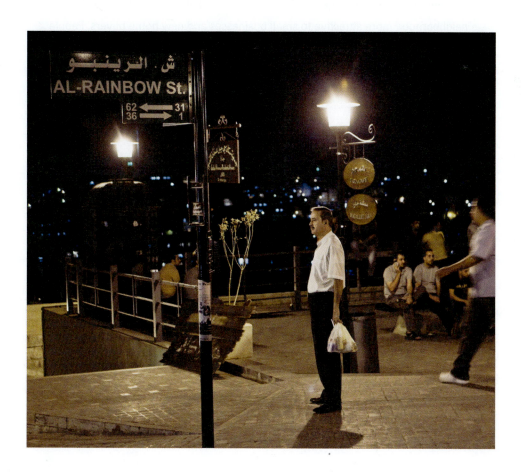

Focused Practice

A. *Work with a partner. Read the thesis statement and the two body paragraphs. Then fill in the examples where they belong in each body paragraph. The first one is done for you.*

Thesis Statement: I support the immediate clean-up of Greenacre Park. This change will improve both the safety and appeal of our neighborhood.

The safety of the community is the main reason why I believe Greenacre should be fixed up. Right now, the park is an eyesore and a dangerous place to be at night. _Many of the park benches are broken, and all of them need painting._ Some of the street lamps don't work. _____ _____

If we fixed the benches and lamps and planted trees, bushes, and flowers, the park would be a more attractive place to be. Improving the park's appearance would encourage more community members to sit out on the benches. This would make Greenacre safer for everyone in the area.

Another reason why it's important to fix up the park is that it will make the neighborhood more attractive to small businesses and new home buyers. People used to like our neighborhood and wanted to live here. _____

_____

_____

_____

Now, every store except the grocery is gone. Store owners and people who want to buy a house no longer want to move here because the park is dangerous and unattractive.

a. There was a coffee shop, a Chinese restaurant, and a grocery store next to the park.

b. Many of the park benches are broken, and all of them need painting.

c. However, when the park became run-down, people stopped shopping and dining out in the area.

d. In addition, many of the trees and flowers have died because of neglect.

B. *Read the following body paragraph. Then fill in the sentence that best concludes the paragraph. Discuss your answer with a partner.*

> One big disadvantage of the changes in Amman is that certain streets have becoming extremely congested and unpleasant to walk on. There are just too many pedestrians, especially along the wide sidewalks of Rainbow and Wakalat Streets. Foot traffic has increased in East Amman because of the new sidewalks and benches. In addition, there are many new stores and restaurants, which bring more people to the area. At busy hours, such as lunchtime and evenings, the crowds come at you like an overpowering wave. It is hard not to run into other people.
>
> _____
>
> _____

a. The automobile traffic on Wakalat Street has now been replaced with foot traffic on its sidewalks.

b. Because there are more nightclubs and restaurants, foot traffic has increased dramatically at night.

c. The changes in Amman have not turned out the way people expected.

d. Instead of encouraging so much foot traffic, Amman should allow people to drive in all parts of the city.

C. *Read the following body paragraph. Work with a partner to write a concluding sentence that sums up the controlling idea. Discuss your answer with another pair of students.*

> Another disadvantage of the new plan is that it might hurt local shop owners. Before the plan, businesses relied on customers who drove right up to their stores. Consumers parked their cars, shopped, and drove away. Shopping was quick and convenient. Now that Wakalat Street is a pedestrian-only street, these shop owners worry about losing loyal customers who are used to parking in front of their storefronts. Some also feel that Wakalat Street has attracted too many young people, who act like wild animals. These teens might scare their customers away. If shopkeepers lose too many customers, they might have to close their shops.
>
> _____
>
> _____

Your Own Writing

Planning Your Body Paragraphs

A. *Before you begin writing your body paragraphs, complete the following outline. Copy your thesis statement from page 84.*

Persuasive Essay

Thesis Statement: _____

_____

_____

▶ Body Paragraph 1

▶ Topic Sentence: _____

    ▶ Supporting Details

        • _____

        • _____

        • _____

    ▶ Summary Sentence (Optional): _____

▶ Body Paragraph 2

▶ Topic Sentence: _____

    ▶ Supporting Details

        • _____

        • _____

        • _____

    ▶ Summary Sentence (Optional): _____

B. Checking in. *Share your outline with a partner. Tell your partner which . . .*

- details you find the most interesting.

- details might need more explanation.

- reason or argument you think is the most convincing and why.

Based on your partner's feedback, you may want to rewrite parts of your outline.

■ THE CONCLUSION

Just as a paragraph usually ends with a concluding sentence that returns to the controlling idea, an essay typically ends with a concluding paragraph that returns to the thesis statement. In the concluding paragraph of an essay, writers return to the idea in the thesis statement in order to leave the reader with a strong impression and clear idea about the topic. They usually restate the thesis in different words. In a persuasive essay about Amman's new plan, for example, you might first sum up whether or not Amman's new plan is a good or a bad change and restate why.

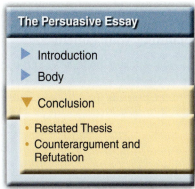

The Persuasive Essay

▶ Introduction
▶ Body
▼ Conclusion
  • Restated Thesis
  • Counterargument and Refutation

In a persuasive essay, you can also end by explaining why the opposing point of view, or counterargument, is not a good one. You can introduce the counterargument with phrases such as these: *Some people believe (that)* or *Some people think (that)*. Then you follow up by refuting, or saying what is wrong with, the opposing view. In this way, you can try to prove that your point of view is stronger than the counterargument.

Here are three strategies you might want to use to end your persuasive essay about a place.

1. Explain why the opposing view, or counterargument, is wrong by reminding readers of the arguments you presented in your thesis statement and topic sentences.

2. Disprove the opposing view, or counterargument, by showing a weakness in it.

3. Remind readers of the reasons for your argument and call for a new action.

Focused Practice

A. *Read the concluding paragraph and answer the questions. Then work with a partner to write one or more concluding sentences.*

> There are two main disadvantages to Amman's new plan. First, it causes too much foot traffic. Second, it can hurt local shop owners. Some people think that the new plan has improved the city. They say the sidewalks have made it feel more friendly and livable. However, not everyone enjoys large crowds. In fact, I think that crowds could make walking through the city even more stressful. When people run into one another, they become upset and overwhelmed. Because such changes can actually make people feel worse, I do not support this new plan.
>
> _____
>
> _____
>
> _____

a. What is the writer's restated thesis? Circle the sentence(s).

b. Which sentences present the counterargument? Underline them.

c. Which sentences refute, or attempt to disprove, the counterargument? Check (✓) them.

Your Own Writing

Planning Your Conclusion

A. *How will you rephrase your thesis statement in the conclusion? List your ideas here.*

_____

_____

B. *What strategy will you use to close the essay?*

_____

_____

C. **Checking in.** *Share your ideas with a partner. Did your partner . . .*

- discover a new and interesting way to return to the thesis statement?
- choose an effective strategy?

Writing Your First Draft

Read the **Tip for Writers.** *Review your notes on pages 81, 84, and 90. Then write the first draft of your essay. When you are finished, give your essay a working title. Hand in your draft to your teacher.*

> **Tip for Writers**
>
> When you write your first draft, be sure to include some descriptive details about the place and proposed change(s).

Step 3   Revising

Revising your work is an essential part of the writing process. This is your opportunity to be sure that your essay has all the important pieces and that it is clear.

Focused Practice

A. *You have read parts of this persuasive essay already. Now read it from beginning to end and notice how the parts fit together.*

The Benefits of the New Amman

Amman, the capital of Jordan, is over 10,000 years old. Today, the city is growing rapidly. Recently, Amman has developed a new plan to change the city. In the past, there weren't many outdoor spaces for the public. Now there are more benches and sidewalks so that people can enjoy the souqs and sights in East Amman and more skyscrapers and fancy restaurants to visit in West Amman. Some

(continued)

Ammanis believe that these changes make the city more livable, but others think they have caused problems. I think that Amman's new plan has benefited the city in two key ways. It has made the city a friendlier place, and it has encouraged diversity.

First of all, the plan has improved Amman's sense of community. Historically, Amman has been divided into two parts. West Amman is the wealthier section and the city's center of business. East Amman is older, more traditional, and less wealthy. They used to be like two different worlds. However, the new plan has brought the rich and poor together in common spaces. On Rainbow and Wakalat Streets, Ammanis and visitors can walk on sidewalks or sit on benches. Because of the benches, people from different backgrounds are more likely to interact with each other face-to-face. I think this makes people in the city feel closer to one another, even to strangers. For example, when someone sits down next to another person, the two might start a conversation. On sidewalks, people say hello and smile at those they pass by. Without public spaces like these, it would be harder to develop a feeling of community in Amman.

Second, the plan has made Amman a more exciting and varied place to be. For visitors and locals, the city is like a feast for the senses. Glass skyscrapers exist close to mosques and churches. People can go to street vendors to buy spicy falafel sandwiches or to McDonald's for a hamburger. They can stroll along concrete streets in the business section or walk along smooth cobblestones on pedestrian-only Wakalat Street. The air is filled with many kinds of sounds, from cars honking their horns to people bargaining for the best price at a local souq. People can buy designer jeans at a fancy clothing store or a handmade bag produced locally. The new plan has brought East and West Amman closer, giving the city a unique mix of old and new. The new plan has made Amman a more vibrant and livable place to be.

Amman's new plan has made the city's people feel more connected to one another. It has highlighted the city's varied architecture and ways of life. There are some people who do not like the changes. For example, local shop owners think the sidewalks are a disadvantage. They say they attract young people, who scare away their customers. However, I think most people have benefited from the changes. A few shopkeepers might lose a sale, but everyone in Amman can enjoy the sidewalks and benches. People belong to a city, but a city should belong to its people too. Cities need to do what is best for the majority of the people, and with its new plan, I think Amman has succeeded in doing this.

B. *Work with a partner. Answer the questions about the essay on page 93.*

1. Which sentences give background information about Amman? Circle them.

2. What is the thesis statement? Underline it.

3. What transition words does the writer use to introduce the topic sentences of the body paragraphs? Double underline them.

4. What supporting details support and develop the controlling idea in each body paragraph? Check (✓) three kinds of support and development in each paragraph.

5. What is the restated thesis? Underline it.

6. Where does the writer refute the opposing view, or counterargument? Circle that section.

C. Checking in. *Discuss your marked-up essays with another pair of students. Then in your group, share one thing about the essay that you found the most interesting. Explain your answer.*

Building Word Knowledge

The writer included two similes in "The Benefits of the New Amman."

Examples:

They [East and West Amman] felt like two different worlds.

The city is like a feast for the senses.

Work with a partner. Circle the two things being compared in each simile. Then work together to write four sentences of your own with similes.

1. The park's newly planted grass glistened like emeralds.

2. Sometimes this street looks as scruffy as an abandoned cat.

3. The local souq was as active as a beehive.

4. The pedestrians' footsteps on the cobblestones sounded like clicking keys on a computer keyboard.

5. The gaping hole in the sidewalk looked like a bad wound.

6. _____

   _____

7. _____

   _____

8. _____

_____

9. _____

_____

10. _____

_____

Your Own Writing

Revising Your Draft

A. *Reread the first draft of your essay. Use the Revision Checklist to identify parts of your writing that might need improvement.*

B. *Review your plans and notes and your responses to the Revision Checklist. Then revise your first draft. Save your revised essay. You will look at it again in the next section.*

Revision Checklist

Did you . . .

☐ express the controlling idea of the whole essay in your thesis statement?

☐ give enough essential background in your introduction?

☐ include descriptive details and opinion markers?

☐ introduce your topic sentences with transition words?

☐ give enough facts, explanations, and examples to support and develop your controlling ideas?

☐ choose to finish your body paragraphs with a summary sentence (or not)?

☐ restate the controlling idea of the essay in your conclusion?

☐ use an effective concluding strategy?

☐ connect the parts of your essay with transition words?

☐ use any similes?

☐ give your essay a good title?

GRAMMAR PRESENTATION

Before you hand in your revised essay, you must check it for any errors in grammar, punctuation, and spelling. In this section, you will learn about the present perfect and the indefinite past. You will focus on this grammar when you edit and proofread your essay.

Present Perfect: Indefinite Past

Grammar Notes	Examples
1. Form the present perfect with: *has / have* + **past participle**	• Trees and sidewalks **have replaced** the streets.
Past participles can be regular or irregular.	• The new plan **has brought** the rich and poor together. • The young people **have scared** his customers away.
The **regular** form of the past participle is: **base form of verb + -d** or **-ed**. This form is the same as the regular simple past form of the verb.	• The city **has turned** into a vibrant gathering place.
BE CAREFUL! There are often spelling changes when you add **-ed** to the verb. There are many irregular past participles.	• The city **has tried** to make Amman a more livable city.

BASE FORM	PAST PARTICIPLE
be	been
bring	brought
do	done
get	gotten
go	gone
have	had
keep	kept
make	made

2. Use the **present perfect** to talk about things that happened at an **indefinite (not exact) time** in the past.	• The city **has removed** most of the benches. *(You don't know exactly when.)*
You can use the present perfect when you <u>don't know</u> when something happened or when the specific time is <u>not important</u>.	• I **have come** to see Amman. *(The specific time isn't important.)*

```
                    Now
                     |
Past ———————X————————|———→ Future
                     |
```

3. Use the **present perfect** with *just* and *recently* to emphasize that something happened in the very recent (but still indefinite) past.

Just goes before the past participle.

Recently can go before the past participle or at the beginning or end of the sentence.

- I have **just** arrived in Amman.

- The city's master plan has **recently** changed all of that.

- Amman has **just** undergone a big change.

- **Recently**, Amman has developed a new plan for the city.

Focused Practice

A. *Circle the correct verb to complete each sentence.*

1. I (**visited / have visited**) Amman, Jordan, with my family in June 2010.

2. Recently, the city (**decided / has decided**) to build a new park.

3. I (**ate / have eaten**) falafel on pita bread many times.

4. Yesterday we (**bought / have bought**) a coral necklace at the local souq.

5. A new restaurant (**opened up / has opened up**) on Wakalat Street.

B. *Read and edit the letter. There are eleven errors in the use of the present perfect, including spelling mistakes. The first error has been corrected for you. Find and correct ten more.*

To the City Officials of Amman,

    I am writing to you about the recent changes that have ~~took~~ *taken* place in our lovely city. I own a clothing store on Wakalat Street. My customers been very loyal to me. However, they are not happy that the city has remove car access to my store. Now they must park farther away. They have complain to me many times, but I have tell them that there is nothing I can do. Now they are complaining about the teenagers who hang out in front of my store. Sometimes the customers who have stoped by the store have feeled uncomfortable. Teenagers often sit on the benches just outside my front door, and they are very loud. I have ask them to be quiet or go someplace else, but they never listen to me. I have did everything I can. I am asking you to help me and my business. Please remove the benches that the city have recently installed on Wakalat Street. Although the benches have made the city more pedestrian friendly, they driven away my loyal customers. I hope you will give my request serious consideration.

                                Sincerely,

                                Adnan Naser

C. *Use the words to write complete sentences about how Wakalat Street has changed. Use the present perfect. The first one is done for you.*

1. The atmosphere of the street / undergo a dramatic change

   The atmosphere of the street has undergone a dramatic change.

2. The city / close Wakalat Street to automobiles

   _____

   _____

3. Wakalat Street / become pedestrian friendly

   _____

   _____

4. Architects / install benches

   _____

   _____

5. City planners / plant trees

   _____

   _____

6. Wakalat Street / develop into a center of activity

   _____

   _____

7. The new design / give Wakalat Street a new identity

   _____

   _____

D. *Write five sentences related to the topic you chose on page 80. Use the* **present perfect.** *These may be sentences you already have in your essay.*

1. _____
   _____

2. _____
   _____

3. _____
   _____

4. _____
   _____

5. _____
   _____

Your Own Writing

Editing Your Draft

A. *Use the Editing Checklist to edit and proofread your essay.*

B. *Prepare a clean copy of the final draft of your essay and hand it in to your teacher.*

Editing Checklist

Did you . . .

☐ include the present perfect and use it correctly?

☐ use correct verb forms, punctuation, and spelling?

☐ use similes and descriptive words correctly?

UNIT 5 Jobs of the Future

IN THIS UNIT You will be writing an essay about the similarities and differences between two jobs.

New technology has opened up many new jobs for people in medicine, business, energy, and the travel industry. As technology continues to change, new jobs will be available and others will no longer be necessary. One exciting area of job growth will be in space tourism. What do you think it would be like to work as a space tour guide?

Planning for Writing

■ BRAINSTORM

A. *Look at the job advertisements. Which of these jobs would you prefer and why? Discuss your answers with a partner.*

TRAVEL IN STYLE

International travel agency looking for experienced agents. 3+ years of experience required. Good computer and people skills a must. Knowledge of world history and several languages a big plus. Should be well traveled in Europe and Asia and have strong sales skills. Competitive salary with commissions and health benefits. Travel discounts available. Part-time position. Email résumé to jobs@travelinstyle.com.

THE FINAL FRONTIER

New space tour company seeking qualified people to guide travelers on 48-hour journeys into space! No experience required, but some astronomy and space science background is essential. Must have good people skills and a sense of adventure. Free four-week mental and physical training offered upon acceptance. Full-time salaried position with flexible schedule. Life and health insurance benefits included. Fax résumé to 800-FRONTIER.

B. **Using a Venn Diagram.** When you write about two topics, you can use a graphic organizer, such as a Venn diagram, to record similarities and differences between them.

Work with a partner. Reread the job ads. Then use the Venn diagram to list similarities and differences between the two jobs.

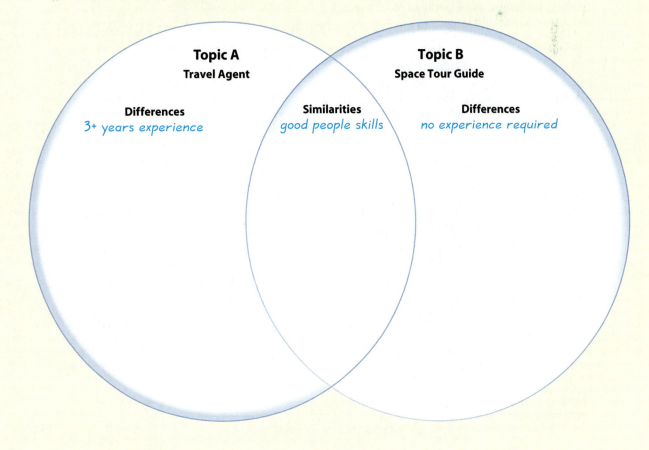

Topic A
Travel Agent

Differences
3+ years experience

Similarities
good people skills

Topic B
Space Tour Guide

Differences
no experience required

Jobs: What the Future Holds

1 Today's workers will have a very different future than their parents and grandparents. Computers, the global economy, and new technologies have all affected the jobs of yesterday, today, and tomorrow. Which jobs are being lost? Which will continue to grow? Take a look into the future and find out.

Bank Tellers

2 When people withdrew money from the bank, they used to talk face-to-face with a bank teller. Today, people do not need a teller to deposit a paycheck anymore. They can find a local ATM machine, which processes the paycheck and gives people everything they need: an updated balance, a receipt, and even cash back.

3 Online banking now puts the job in everyone else's hands. Need to transfer money? Done. Check your balance? No problem—it's just a click away. As online banking becomes more popular, the future of bank tellers is uncertain.

Machine Operators

4 People depend on machines and tools to make the products they use every day, from car parts to toasters. With the world population getting bigger by the minute, won't we need more machine operators to run the machines?

5 Unfortunately, the answer is no. More factories are replacing human operators with robots and computer-controlled machine tools. Robots can work longer and make more accurate repairs. And they don't need a paycheck. Robots save companies a lot of time and money, but the drawback is a big one: the loss of many jobs for machine operators.

Travel Agents

6 Not long ago, people went to a travel agent to book[1] their vacations. Since the invention of the Internet, all of that has changed.

7 Now travelers can find out about vacation spots, compare flight times and prices, and book hotels on their own. Travel agents are not going away completely, but they have stiff[2] competition thanks (or not thanks) to the World Wide Web.

International Business Consultants

8 Attention to those of you who are good with numbers and speak a foreign language—more and more jobs are coming your way. Experts predict a 20 percent increase in the next 10 years for international business consultants (IBCs). Companies need IBCs to help them decide on the best places to do business in foreign countries. As more companies take advantage of the global economy, IBCs will be in even greater demand.

Renewable Energy Technicians

9 Green jobs[3] are red hot. Jobs in protecting and improving the environment are growing rapidly. This is where the renewable energy (RE) technician comes in.

10 More and more countries are using renewable energy sources, such as solar power and wind power. Consequently, they will need RE technicians to install and repair

---

[1] **book:** to arrange to stay at a hotel, fly on a plane, etc., at a particular time in the future
[2] **stiff:** more difficult, strict, or severe than usual
[3] **green jobs:** jobs related to or concerned about the environment

their solar panels and wind turbines.[4] That is why renewable energy is expected to become one of the fastest growing industries of the future.

11 Space Tour Guides

Do you love to travel? Do you want to get paid to explore unknown places? A job as a space tour guide may be the answer. With today's advanced aircraft, space travel is already a reality. Virgin Galactic promises to take people 60 miles above the earth, where they will experience zero gravity. Space Adventures has already taken people to the International Space Station—at $20 million per person.

12 Today there are a number of space tourism companies that need tour guides to bring outer space to life. It might be a risky job, but the benefits are huge. You not only get to experience life above Earth—you also get paid for doing so. Here's to the future!

---

[4] **turbines:** engines that work when the pressure from a liquid or gas moves special wheels around

Building Word Knowledge

Using Collocations. To write well, select words and expressions that express your meaning accurately and naturally. In English, certain words appear together frequently. These word partners are called *collocations*. Here are some collocations from "Jobs: What the Future Holds."

global economy: the way that money, businesses, and products are organized throughout the whole world

world population: the total number of people living in the world

green jobs: types of work that are related to or concerned with the environment

renewable energy: energy that is able to be replaced by natural processes so that it is never used up

Locate the collocations in the reading on page 102. Notice how they are used.

Focused Practice

A. *Read the* Tip for Writers. *Work with a partner. Discuss the writer's main purpose for writing "Jobs: What the Future Holds." Then, on your own, write a sentence explaining what the writer's purpose is and how you know this.*

_____

_____

B. *Read the article again. Write the name of the job and circle* an increase *or* a decrease *to complete each statement based on the reading. The first one is done for you.*

1. ATMs and online banking are causing (**an increase** / **a decrease**) in jobs for

   _____bank tellers_____.

2. Factory use of robots is causing (**an increase** / **a decrease**) in jobs for

   _____.

> **Tip for Writers**
>
> Before writers begin to write about a topic, they have to determine their **purpose** for writing. The purpose affects how and what they discuss about the topic. There are three basic purposes for writing: to inform, to persuade, or to entertain.

(continued)

3. Use of solar and wind power is causing (**an increase / a decrease**) in jobs for

_____.

4. The global economy is causing (**an increase / a decrease**) in jobs for

_____.

5. The Internet is causing (**an increase / a decrease**) in jobs for _____.

6. Advanced aircraft is causing (**an increase / a decrease**) in jobs for

_____.

C. _Work with a partner. Look at the list of jobs from the reading. What inferences (or good guesses) can you make about the skills that each job requires? Check (✓) your answers. Discuss your answers with another pair of students._

	Math Skills	Technical Skills	People Skills
1. Bank teller			
2. Machine operator			
3. Travel agent			
4. International business consultant			
5. Renewable energy technician			
6. Space tour guide			

D. _Choose two of the jobs from Exercise C. Which of the two jobs do you think is more exciting? Write a paragraph explaining why._

_____

_____

_____

_____

_____

_____

Writing a Compare-Contrast Essay

You are going to write an essay that compares and contrasts two jobs. When you compare, you show how two people or things are alike. When you contrast, you show how they are different. A compare-contrast essay describes how two people or things are alike or different in specific ways.

Like all essays, a compare-contrast essay contains three parts.

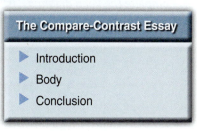

The Compare-Contrast Essay

▶ Introduction

▶ Body

▶ Conclusion

Step 1   Prewriting

For a compare-contrast essay, the prewriting step involves selecting two people or things that have clear similarities and/or differences. It also includes brainstorming ideas to develop specific points of comparison and contrast. We'll use the phrase *points of comparison* to mean points of contrast as well.

Your Own Writing

Choosing Your Assignment

A. *Choose Assignment 1 or Assignment 2.*

   1. Compare and contrast two jobs you are interested in. Then comment on which job would be best for you, based on your skills and interests.

   2. Interview two people with different jobs. Compare and contrast the work they do. Then express your opinion about which job is more interesting.

B. *Freewrite for 10 minutes on your assignment. Here are some questions to get you started:*

   • What do you already know about the two jobs?

   • Why are these jobs interesting to you?

   • What more do you want to find out about them?

C. **Checking in.** *Work with a partner who chose the same assignment. Discuss the ideas you just wrote. Did your partner . . .*

   • choose two jobs that have clear similarities and/or differences?

   • describe ways in which the jobs are alike or different?

   • express an opinion about the job he or she prefers or finds more interesting?

Share your opinions about your partner's comparison. Based on your discussion, make changes and additions to your writing. ➡

D. *Complete the Venn diagram. List the similarities and differences between the two jobs. Fill in as much information as you can. You will have a chance to review, change, or add information later in the unit.*

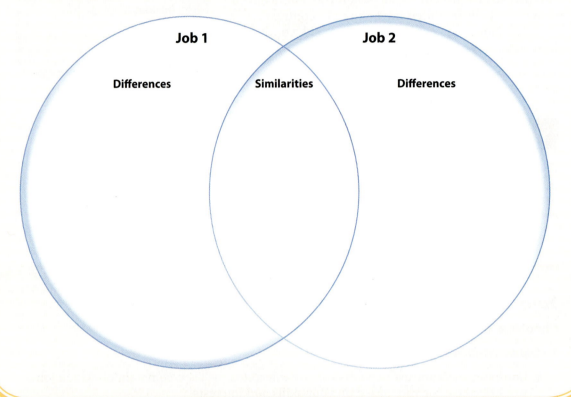

Step 2   Writing the First Draft

■ THE INTRODUCTION

As you learned in Unit 4, the introductory paragraph in an essay contains two parts:

1. **Background information** about the topic of the essay to help your reader to understand and become interested in the topic.

2. A **thesis statement** that presents the controlling idea of the essay.

In a compare-contrast essay, the thesis statement usually states the two topics being compared and contrasted and the important points of comparison. It may be one sentence or two sentences.

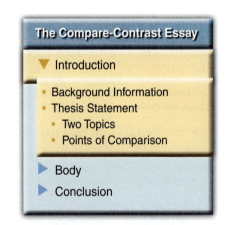

The Compare-Contrast Essay

▼ Introduction
  • Background Information
  • Thesis Statement
    • Two Topics
    • Points of Comparison

▶ Body
▶ Conclusion

Example:

topic #1   topic #2   controlling idea
Bank tellers and international business consultants differ in two important ways. They

point of comparison #1   point of comparison #2
have different salaries and work in different environments.

Focused Practice

A. *Read the following essay assignment. Then decide which details you might use as background information for an introductory paragraph on this topic. Check (✓) the sentences you choose. Discuss your answers with a partner.*

Compare and contrast the jobs of a travel agent and a space tour guide.

_____ **1.** Jobs in the travel industry are for people who like travel and adventure.

_____ **2.** I would like to be a space tour guide.

_____ **3.** Most people need to have a job.

_____ **4.** Soon, people who like adventure will be able to work as space tour guides.

_____ **5.** Advances in technology have opened up new jobs in space tourism.

_____ **6.** In the past, many travel lovers became travel agents.

B. *Read the following essay assignment and sentences. Then check (✓) the sentences that would make good thesis statements for an essay on this topic. Discuss your answers with a partner.*

Compare and contrast two jobs that have some similarities and differences.

_____ **1.** Travel agents and travel writers both study people and places in other parts of the world. However, the skills needed for each job are different.

_____ **2.** Lawyers have a job that is unique and highly paid but very stressful.

_____ **3.** Doctors earn more money than nurses, but being a nurse is more satisfying.

_____ **4.** Pharmacists can work in either a hospital or a retail pharmacy.

_____ **5.** Veterinarians and zoologists both enjoy working with animals; however, vets take care of animals, and zoologists study wild animals.

_____ **6.** Engineers have to be good in two subjects: math and physics.

_____ **7.** Both renewable energy technicians and machine operators must have excellent technical and problem-solving skills.

_____ **8.** Although actors and directors both work on films, they use different skills and perform different kinds of roles.

C. *Read the model introductory paragraph for the following essay assignment. Then discuss the questions on page 108 with a partner.*

Compare and contrast the jobs of a travel agent and a space tour guide.

Jobs in the travel industry are for people who like travel and adventure. In the past, many travel lovers became travel agents. Today, advances in technology have opened up new jobs in space tourism. Soon, people who like adventure will be able to work as space tour guides. For people considering jobs as either travel agents or space tour guides, there are important points to consider. Despite a few similarities, the jobs of a travel agent and a space tour guide are very different. The training needed for each job is different, as are the work environments.

1. Which ideas from Exercise A did the writer include as background?

2. Why do you think the writer used some ideas but not others?

3. What is the writer's thesis statement?

4. What two points of comparison do you expect the essay to cover?

5. Does the first sentence of the introduction interest you in the topic? Why or why not?

Your Own Writing

Finding Out More

A. *Go online or to the library to learn more about the two jobs you chose to compare and contrast for your essay.*

- Find out more about the skills and qualifications that are important for the job, including the salary, the work environment, and the job outlook (whether these jobs will be available in the future).

- You may want to use the following keywords when you search for information online: *future jobs, jobs in 2020,* or *hot jobs for the future.*

B. *Take notes on what you found out. List key information about each job and be sure to note key information on your sources. (See the Appendix on pages 150–151.) Add new points of comparison or contrast to the Venn diagram on page 106. Use this information when you write your essay.*

C. Checking in. *Share your information with your partner, and give each other feedback. Did your partner . . .*

- gather enough job-related facts and details?

- use at least three reliable sources?

Planning Your Introduction

A. *List the background information you will need to include in your introduction.*

_____

_____

_____

B. *Write a draft of your thesis statement. Make sure your thesis statement clearly states the two jobs and the points of comparison your essay will discuss. Look back at your freewriting and Venn diagram to help you.*

_____

_____

■ THE BODY

When you wrote your four-paragraph essay in Unit 4, you used your two body paragraphs to present and develop ideas in support of your thesis statement. Now you will write a four-paragraph compare-contrast essay. There are two ways to organize the body paragraphs of a compare-contrast essay: the *block method* or *point-by-point*.

In the block method, you discuss all of the points of comparison about the first person, thing, or idea. Then you discuss the same points of comparison, usually in the same order, about the second person, thing, or idea. In the point-by-point method, you discuss each point of comparison about the two people, things, or ideas one at a time.

Example:

Thesis Statement: Despite a few similarities, the jobs of a travel agent and a space tour guide are very different. The training needed for each job is different, as are the work environments.

Block Method

I.   Paragraph 1: Introduction

II. Paragraph 2: Travel Agent

    A. Training required

    B. Work environment

III. Paragraph 3: Space Tour Guide

    A. Training required

    B. Work environment

IV. Paragraph 4: Conclusion

Point-by-Point Method

I.   Paragraph 1: Introduction

II. Paragraph 2: Training Required

    A. Travel agent

    B. Space tour guide

III. Paragraph 3: Work Environment

    A. Travel agent

    B. Space tour guide

IV. Paragraph 4: Conclusion

Writing Topic Sentences

As you learned in Unit 4, body paragraphs usually begin with a topic sentence that clearly states the controlling idea of the paragraph without using the same words as the thesis statement. You also learned that topic sentences in body paragraphs often begin with listing-order transition words such as *first of all*, *second*, and *in addition*.

The topic sentence in each body paragraph of a point-by-point compare–contrast essay introduces one point of comparison. Writers may use compare–contrast transition words, including the ones in the chart, to signal the point of comparison.

Comparisons	Contrasts
another similarity	although
both	but
like	however
one similarity	one difference
similarly	on the other hand
	unlike

Example:

Thesis Statement: The qualifications and work settings for bank tellers and international business consultants include similarities and differences.

Topic Sentence 1: First of all, both tellers and international business consultants must have excellent math skills.

Topic Sentence 2: On the other hand, tellers and international business consultants often work in very different environments.

Focused Practice

Read the thesis statements. Topic Sentence 1 for each thesis statement is already written. Write what Topic Sentence 2 should be. Use the ideas and transition words in parentheses to help you.

1. **Thesis Statement:** *Veterinarians and zoologists both enjoy working with animals; however, vets take care of animals, and zoologists study wild animals.*

   Topic Sentence 1: *Like a veterinarian, a zoologist must have a strong interest in animals.*

   Topic Sentence 2: *(Idea: Vets are concerned with the health of pets; zoologists study behavior of all kinds of animals. Transition word:* while*)*

   _____

   _____

2. **Thesis Statement:** *Although actors and directors both need to know how movies are made, they use different skills and perform different jobs.*

   Topic Sentence 1: *First of all, like directors, actors need to learn the steps in making movies.*

Topic Sentence 2: (*Idea: Actors must learn how to play a character and memorize lines; directors manage all aspects of a film. Transition word:* however)

_____

_____

Developing a Body Paragraph

In Unit 4, you learned that the topic sentence of each body paragraph must be developed and supported. In a compare-contrast essay, you explain and/or describe how two people, things, or ideas are similar and/or different so that the reader understands your points of comparison. Then you support each point of comparison with evidence, such as facts and examples. Transition words will help you connect the sentences in your body paragraph to each other and back to your topic sentence.

Focused Practice

A. *On page 107, you read an introductory paragraph for a compare-contrast essay about travel agents and space tour guides. Now read the writer's thesis statement again and the first body paragraph. Then discuss the questions with a partner.*

> **Thesis Statement:** Despite a few similarities, the jobs of a travel agent and a space tour guide are very different. The training for each job is different, as are the work environments.
>
> First of all, although travel agents and space tour guides both need to go to school, the type of training they need is different. Travel agents usually go to community colleges or travel industry schools. They learn how to make travel arrangements, including airline and hotel reservations. They learn about travel documents, such as passports and visas. Some also study geography, history, and foreign languages. Unlike travel agents, space tour guides will probably have to learn more than geography and history. They will most likely need to study space science, including astronomy. In addition, they will need special mental and physical training, as astronauts do. They will have to deal with weightlessness, lack of sleep, and other hard parts of space travel.

1. What is the controlling idea of the paragraph? Underline it.

2. What differences does the paragraph present about travel agents and space tour guides? Circle the transition words the writer uses to contrast.

3. What supporting details does the paragraph present? List three details for each job.

Travel Agents: _____

Space Tour Guides: _____

B. *Work with a partner. Read the thesis statement and the examples. Then fill in the two examples with the phrases that best complete each body paragraph. The first one is done for you.*

1.

Thesis Statement: Veterinarians and zoologists both enjoy working with animals; however, vets take care of animals and zoologists study wild animals.

A major difference between veterinarians and zoologists is the type of work they do with animals. The main job of veterinarians is to keep pets healthy and heal sick or injured domestic animals. For example, *veterinarians give dogs and cats vaccinations and take care of the pets' teeth* .

Unlike a veterinarian, a zoologist studies the behavior, diseases, and life cycles of wild animals. Zoologists gather scientific information about animal behavior and habits, including the effects that human beings have on wildlife. They research the effects of environmental change on wildlife. For example,

_____

_____.

a. a zoologist might study how global warming is affecting polar bears

b. veterinarians give dogs and cats vaccinations and take care of the pets' teeth

c. veterinarians and zoologists both have to go to college

d. a zoologist doesn't know how to care for dogs and cats

2.

Thesis Statement: Although actors and directors both need to know how movies are made, they use different skills and perform different jobs.

One difference between actors and directors is the specific job they perform in the making of a film. Actors focus on the characters they are playing. For example,

_____

_____.

However, directors manage all of the creative parts of a movie. They hold rehearsals and comment on how the actors are playing their parts. In addition,

_____

_____.

a. they must learn their lines and try to act like the characters they are playing

b. they must know and like the director of the film

c. they make decisions about the setting, costumes, and lighting

d. they get paid a higher salary than actors do

Your Own Writing

Planning Your Body Paragraphs

A. *You are going to organize your essay according to the point-by-point method. Before you begin writing your body paragraphs, complete the following outline. Copy your thesis statement from page 108.*

Compare-Contrast Essay

Thesis Statement: _____

_____

▶ Body Paragraph 1

  ▶ Topic Sentence: _____

    _____

    ▶ Job 1: Supporting Details

      • _____

      • _____

      • _____

    ▶ Job 2: Supporting Details

      • _____

      • _____

      • _____

▶ Body Paragraph 2

  ▶ Topic Sentence: _____

    _____

    ▶ Job 1: Supporting Details:

      • _____

      • _____

      • _____

➡️

▶ Job 2: Supporting Details

- _____
- _____
- _____

B. Checking in. *Share your outline with a partner. Tell your partner which . . .*

- details you find the most interesting.
- details might need more explanation.
- point of comparison your partner should discuss first and why.
- point of comparison your partner should discuss second and why.

Based on your partner's feedback, you may want to rewrite parts of your outline.

■ THE CONCLUSION

As you learned in Unit 4, the conclusion is where you wrap up or close your essay. You usually return to the controlling idea in the thesis statement in order to leave the reader with a strong impression. Some writers include transition words to let readers know that the conclusion is beginning, for example, *in conclusion, to sum up, in sum*, and *in summary*. Other writers leave these words out. The choice is yours.

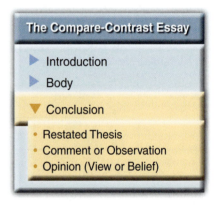

In an essay comparing travel agents and space tour guides, you might first sum up the differences between the two jobs. Then you could express an opinion about which job you would enjoy most and explain why. Your conclusion doesn't have to be very long—it just has to be long enough to return to your thesis statement and end in an interesting and clear way.

Here are two strategies you might want to use to end your compare-contrast essay about two jobs:

1. Look to the future of the two jobs and comment on it.

2. Present an opinion about which job is more exciting or fitting for you.

Focused Practice

Read the model of a concluding paragraph and answer the questions.

> In conclusion, travel agents and space tour guides have different kinds of
>
> training and work environments. Because of this, the life of a travel agent is
>
> *(continued)*

best for people who like to travel but don't like danger. To be a space tour guide, you must not only like to travel. You must also be comfortable with extreme experiences and a risky job. Although I'd love to be able to see Earth from space, I wouldn't enjoy the dangers of blasting off into space. I would rather keep my feet on the ground!

1. Where does the writer restate the thesis? Underline the statement.

2. What transition words does the writer use to signal that this is the conclusion? Circle them.

3. What concluding strategy does the writer use? _____

Your Own Writing

Planning Your Conclusion

A. *How will you rephrase your thesis statement in the conclusion? List your ideas here.*

_____

_____

B. *What strategy will you use to close the essay?*

_____

_____

C. Checking in. *Share your ideas with a partner. Did your partner . . .*

- discover a new and interesting way to rephrase the thesis?
- choose an effective strategy?

Writing Your First Draft

Read the Tip for Writers. *Review your notes on pages 106, 108, and 113. Then write the first draft of your essay. When you are finished, give your essay a working title. Hand in your draft to your teacher.*

Tip for Writers

When you write your first draft, be sure that the purpose of your essay is clear.

Revising your work is an essential part of the writing process. This is your opportunity to be sure that your essay has all the important pieces and that it is clear.

Focused Practice

A. *You have read parts of this compare-contrast essay already. Now read it from beginning to end and notice how the parts fit together.*

Where to Keep My Feet

Jobs in the travel industry are for people who like travel and adventure. In the past, many travel lovers became travel agents. Today, advances in technology have opened up new jobs in space tourism. Soon, people who like adventure will be able to work as space tour guides. For people considering jobs as either travel agents or space tour guides, there are important points to consider. Despite a few similarities, the jobs of a travel agent and a space tour guide are very different. The training needed for each job is different, as are the work environments.

First of all, although travel agents and space tour guides both need to go to school, the type of training they need is different. Travel agents usually go to community colleges or travel industry schools. They learn how to make travel arrangements, including airline and hotel reservations. They learn about travel documents, such as passports and visas. Some also study geography, history, and foreign languages. Unlike travel agents, space tour guides will probably need to learn more than geography and history. They will most likely need to study space science, including astronomy. In addition, they will need special mental and physical training, as astronauts do. They will have to deal with weightlessness, lack of sleep, and other hard parts of space travel.

Secondly, the places where travel agents and space tour guides work are very different. Travel agents spend most of their time at a desk. Some work in an office or travel agency; others are self-employed and work at home. Travel agents may never meet some of their customers. They work pretty regular hours, and their work environments are safe. In contrast, space tour guides work on a small spaceship and must put in longer periods of time in that cramped place. Like airline attendants, space tour guides will have to deal day and night with all of the travelers on the ship. They will need to provide food, comfort, and entertainment for the space tourists. Even if space travel becomes safer, working in space will still be much riskier than working at a desk job.

(continued)

In conclusion, travel agents and space tour guides have different kinds of training and work environments. Because of this, the life of a travel agent is best for people who like to travel but don't like danger. To be a space tour guide, you must not only like to travel. You must also be comfortable with extreme experiences and a risky job. Although I'd love to be able to see Earth from space, I wouldn't enjoy the dangers of blasting off into space. I would rather keep my feet on the ground!

B. *Work with a partner. Answer the questions about the essay.*

1. What is the thesis statement? Underline it.

2. What is the main point of comparison in Paragraph 2? Underline the sentence that states it.

3. What is the main point of comparison in Paragraph 3? Underline the sentence that states it.

4. What transition words connect the parts of the essay? Circle them.

5. What facts, details, and examples support and develop the controlling idea in each body paragraph? Check (✓) three kinds of support and development in each paragraph.

6. Where does the writer express a personal opinion? Put an X next to it.

C. Checking in. *Discuss your marked-up essays with another pair of students. Then in your group, share one thing about the essay that you found the most interesting. Explain your answer.*

Building Word Knowledge

The writer included many job-related collocations in "Where to Keep My Feet," including *work environment, travel industry, travel agents, travel arrangements, space travel,* and *tour guides.*

Work with a partner. Use each word from the box to form two collocations. Sometimes the word comes first, and sometimes it comes second.

insurance	music	services	skills	technology

1. _____insurance_____ agent   homeowner's _____insurance_____

2. information _____   advanced _____

3. people _____   spelling _____

4. _____ industry   _____ business

5. health-care _____   public _____

Your Own Writing

Revising Your Draft

A. *Reread the first draft of your essay. Use the Revision Checklist to identify parts of your writing that might need improvement.*

B. *Review your plans and notes and your responses to the Revision Checklist. Then revise your first draft. Save your revised essay. You will look at it again in the next section.*

Revision Checklist

Did you . . .

☐ express the controlling idea of the whole essay in your thesis statement?

☐ give enough essential background in your introduction?

☐ make the purpose of your essay clear?

☐ present a main point of comparison in each body paragraph?

☐ give enough supporting facts, details, and examples?

☐ restate the controlling idea of the essay in your conclusion?

☐ use an effective concluding strategy?

☐ connect the parts of your essay with transition words?

☐ use any collocations in your essay?

☐ give your essay a good title?

■ GRAMMAR PRESENTATION

Before you hand in your revised essay, you must check it for any errors in grammar, punctuation, and spelling. In this section, you will learn about comparative adjectives. You will focus on this grammar when you edit and proofread your essay.

Adjectives: Comparisons with *As . . . as* and *Than*

Grammar Notes	Examples
1. Use *(not) as* + **adjective** + *as* to compare people, places, or things and show how they are (or aren't) **similar**:	**A:** Nurses are **as important as** doctors. **B:** But a nurse's salary is **not as high as** a doctor's salary.
a. Use *as* + **adjective** + *as* to show how they are <u>the same or equal</u>. Use *just* to make the comparison stronger.	• A nurse's job is *just* **as hard as** a doctor's job.
b. Use *(not) as* + **adjective** + *as* to show how they are <u>not the same or equal</u>.	• A nurse's job is **not as technical as** a doctor's.
2. Use **comparative adjectives** + *than* to show how people, places, or things are **different**.	• The job of an international business consultant is **harder than** that of a bank teller. • A consultant's salary is **more competitive than** a bank teller's.
3. There are several ways of **forming comparative adjectives**:	

	ADJECTIVE	COMPARATIVE
a. For **short adjectives** (one-syllable and two-syllable ending in *-y*), use **adjective** + *-er*	fast friendly	faster friendlier
There are often **spelling changes** when you add *-er*	free big happy	fre**er** big**ger** happ**ier**
Some adjectives have **irregular** comparative forms.	good bad	**better** **worse**
b. For **long adjectives** (two or more syllables), use *more / less* + **adjective**	skillful	more skillful less skillful

c. For **some adjectives**, such as *lively*, *quiet*, and *risky*, you can use either *-er* or *more*

• Leading space tours is **riskier** than making travel arrangements.
• Leading space tours is **more risky** than making travel arrangements.

(continued)

4. Use **than** before the second part of the comparison.	• My job is **harder than** her job.	
REMEMBER: It's not necessary to mention both parts of the comparison when the meaning is clear.	• My new job is **better**. *(than my old job)*	
5. Comparatives with **than** and comparisons with **as . . . as** often express the <u>same meaning</u> in different ways.	• My job is **more difficult than** her job. • Her job **isn't as difficult as** my job. • Her job is **less difficult than** my job.	
USAGE NOTE: With <u>one-syllable adjectives</u>, **not as . . . as** is more common than **less . . . than**.	• Her salary isn't **as high as** mine.	

Focused Practice

A. *Look at the comment cards from customers who recently spoke to a travel agent at* Travel in Style. *Compare the two travel agents. Then complete the sentences on page 121. Use* as . . . as *or* not as . . . as *and the correct form of the word in parentheses.*

COMMENT CARD

AGENT NAME: *Christine*

	Poor	Fair	Good	Excellent
1. How fast was your agent?	○	○	☑	○
2. How helpful was your agent?	○	☑	○	○
3. How friendly was your agent?	○	☑	○	○
4. How knowledgeable was your agent?	○	○	○	☑
5. How accurate was your agent?	○	○	☑	○
6. How polite was your agent?	☑	○	○	○

COMMENT CARD

AGENT NAME: *Ruth*

	Poor	Fair	Good	Excellent
1. How fast was your agent?	○	○	☑	○
2. How helpful was your agent?	○	○	☑	○
3. How friendly was your agent?	○	○	○	☑
4. How knowledgeable was your agent?	○	○	○	☑
5. How accurate was your agent?	○	○	○	☑
6. How polite was your agent?	○	○	☑	○

1. Christine was _____as fast as_____ (**fast**) Ruth.

2. Christine was _____ (**helpful**) Ruth.

3. Christine was _____ (**friendly**) Ruth.

4. Ruth was _____ (**knowledgeable**) Christine.

5. Ruth was _____ (**accurate**) Christine.

6. Christine was _____ (**polite**) Ruth.

B. *Look at the chart comparing two popular vacation spots: Rio de Janeiro, Brazil, and Honolulu, Hawaii, USA. Complete the sentences comparing the two places. Use the appropriate comparative form of the adjectives in parentheses and* **than**.

	Rio de Janeiro, Brazil	Honolulu, Hawaii, USA
Population	6,186,710	905,034
Average temperature	24°C / 75°F	25°C / 77°F
Sunny days per year	300	271
Average rainfall	109 cm / 43 in.	99 cm / 39 in.
Average hotel cost	$100 / night	$175 / night
Cost of a cup of coffee	$0.82	$3.00

1. Honolulu is _____ (**populous**) than Rio de Janeiro.

2. The average temperature in Honolulu is slightly _____ (**warm**) than

the temperature in Rio de Janeiro.

3. Rio de Janeiro is _____ (**sunny**) than Honolulu.

4. Honolulu is _____ (**dry**) than Rio de Janeiro.

5. A hotel in Honolulu is _____ (**expensive**) than one in Rio de Janeiro.

6. A cup of coffee in Rio is _____ (**cheap**) than one in Honolulu.

C. *Compare and contrast a vacation to Rio de Janeiro with one to Honolulu. Which destination would you prefer and why? Discuss your choice with a partner. Use the comparative adjectives from Exercise B in your discussion.*

D. *Read and edit the paragraph. There are eight errors in the use of comparative adjectives. The first error has been corrected for you. Find and correct seven more.*

>   *than*
>   The job of a space tour guide is more difficult ~~as~~ working as a travel agent.
> A tour guide has to work in more riskier conditions than an agent. Traveling into
> space is a much dangerous and complicated process than booking vacation
> packages. Tour guides need to be able to stay calmer at all times. In addition, they
> must make the passengers feel safe. The job of a travel agent is a lot less difficult
> and not nearly dangerous as that of a space tour guide. A travel agent's work
> environment is peacefuler and comfortable. Travel agents do not need to worry
> about the physical safety of their clients, which makes their job more easier to do.
> However, I like challenges, so a job as a space tour guide would be a more better
> job for me.

E. *Write five sentences related to the topic you chose on page 105.* Use *comparative adjectives.*
These may be sentences you already have in your essay.

1. _____

   _____

2. _____

   _____

3. _____

   _____

4. _____

   _____

5. _____

   _____

Your Own Writing

Editing Your Draft

A. *Use the Editing Checklist to edit and proofread your essay.*

B. *Prepare a clean copy of the final draft of your essay and hand it in to your teacher.*

Editing Checklist

Did you . . .

☐ include comparative adjectives and use them correctly?

☐ use correct verb forms, punctuation, and spelling?

☐ use collocations and other words correctly?

UNIT 6 Staying Healthy

IN THIS UNIT   You will be writing an essay about a health problem and its solution.

For centuries, doctors have stressed the importance of hygiene, or keeping ourselves clean to avoid illnesses. People used to use only soap and water to stay clean. Now many people carry alcohol-based hand sanitizers with them wherever they go to get rid of germs. When cleanliness doesn't work, we have to rely on our immune system, our natural defense system that helps the body get over a sickness. We also take antibiotics, which are medicines that fight bacteria. What do you do to stay healthy? How do you prevent illnesses?

Planning for Writing

■ BRAINSTORM

A. *Take the hygiene test below using your own knowledge. Discuss your answers with a partner. Check your answers below.*

B. *Read the questions about health habits. Discuss your answers with a partner.*

   1. What do you do to keep yourself healthy?

   2. What do you do to treat the common cold?

   3. When you get sick, do you take medicine or use natural remedies?

C. **Using a Problem-Solution Chart.** When you write about a problem, you can use a problem-solution chart to describe what the problem is, why it is a problem, and how it might be solved.

Work with a partner. Read the health problems in column 1 of the chart. Then in column 2, write three possible solutions to each problem.

> **1.** To kill germs, people should wash their hands for.
>   **a.** 5 seconds
>   **b.** 10 seconds
>   **c.** 30 seconds
>
> **2.** An alcohol-based hand sanitizer kills germs better than soap and water.
>   **a.** True
>   **b.** False
>
> **3.** People should take antibiotics _____.
>   **a.** whenever they get sick
>   **b.** for a high fever
>   **c.** only when necessary
>
> Answers: 1. c; 2. b; 3 c.

Problem (and Why it Is One)	Possible Solutions
1. Many people suffer from the flu and the common cold, and these illnesses are hard to prevent, especially during the winter.	*Be sure to get enough rest.*
2. Ear infections are painful, and they can be very hard to get rid of.	
3. Asthma and other allergic reactions can be dangerous, and they are more and more common today.	

The Hygiene Hypothesis[1]

1   In today's world, more people have easy access to medicines than ever before. At the same time, there are more products to help keep us and our surroundings clean, from antibacterial[2] sprays to germ-killing[3] soaps to hand sanitizers.[4] However, recent medical research suggests that keeping ourselves and our environment very clean might not be the road to better health.

A New Germ Theory

2   Immunologists are scientists who study the effect of germs on our bodies. They have determined that some germs *do* make us sick, but not all germs are bad. The body needs certain germs to carry out important functions. For example, some bacteria are needed to help the stomach digest[5] food. Others help the body fight disease. According to these scientists, people may not be getting enough germs to stay healthy.

3   This is the basis for the *hygiene hypothesis*.[6] It states that we cannot fight off common germs when the body and environment are *too* clean. The immune system, which controls how the body fights diseases, cannot develop properly without germs. If we are not exposed to enough germs, it ends up losing strength. Therefore, we get sick more easily.

Antibiotics and Superbugs

4   Antibiotics are medicines that kill bacteria and help us fight bacterial illnesses. However, researchers in Israel have found that not prescribing[7] antibiotics may improve patients' health. When patients took fewer antibiotics in the summer months, they also ended up having fewer ear infections. Why was this the case?

5   When scientists developed antibiotics in the 1940s, many doctors, especially in the United States, prescribed them for all kinds of illnesses, including sore throats and the common cold. After a while, some kinds of

bacteria changed. These germs became resistant to antibiotic treatment—that is, the antibiotics no longer worked. When people got sick from these newer bacteria, the antibiotics could not kill them anymore. Because the bacteria were so powerful, doctors called them *superbugs*. Today, 70 percent of hospital deaths in the United States are caused by these hard-to-treat superbugs. To avoid creating more superbugs, doctors are now encouraged to prescribe antibiotics only when absolutely necessary.

---

[1] **hypothesis:** an idea that is suggested as an explanation of something but has not yet been proved to be true

[2] **antibacterial:** used in order to kill bacteria that cause infections

[3] **germ-killing:** able to kill a very small living thing that can make you ill

[4] **sanitizers:** chemical substances such as alcohol that kill germs

[5] **digest:** to change food in the stomach into a form your body can use

[6] **hygiene hypothesis:** a to-be-proven theory about the unhealthy effects of excessive cleanliness

[7] **prescribing:** saying what medicine or treatment a sick person should have

Siblings,[8] Dogs, and Allergies

6   According to a study by Norwegian and British scientists, too much cleanliness may also bring about disease. If the body does not encounter enough germs in the environment, the immune system can begin to attack itself. This can cause immune-related diseases, such as hay fever, asthma, and other allergies.

7   The scientists looked at 14,000 adults in New Zealand, Australia, the United States, and Europe. They found that children in larger families were healthier. Having more siblings kept their immune systems busier because there were more germs around. The same was true for children who shared a bedroom or grew up with a dog. Siblings and pets helped prevent the immune system from attacking itself. As a result, the children ended up with fewer allergies.

Being Less Clean

8   Studies on antibiotics and germless environments have helped support the hygiene hypothesis. More scientists agree that a healthy immune system needs the right balance of good and bad germs. But they are still trying to figure out what the correct balance is and how to control it.

9   Today's scientists are looking for a solution to this problem. One solution is offered by Tore Midvedt. Midvedt is a scientist at the Karolinska Institute in Sweden who studies good and bad germs. He believes that the simplest solution is to expose yourself to more germs. "I'm not saying that we should be more dirty," says Midvedt, "I'm saying we should be less clean."

_____

[8] siblings: brothers or sisters

Building Word Knowledge

Using Phrasal Verbs. Many verbs in English have a different meaning when they are combined with other words. *Phrasal verbs* are verbs that are followed by a particle, such as *about, for, off, out, up,* and *with*. These verbs have a different or more specific meaning than the verb used on its own. Here are some examples of phrasal verbs from "The Hygiene Hypothesis." Notice how their meanings are different from the meanings of the verbs (*bring, carry, end, fight, figure, look*).

bring about: to make something happen

carry out: to do something that needs to be organized or controlled

end up: to be in a particular situation, especially when you did not plan it

fight off: to try hard to get rid of something, especially an illness

figure out: to think about a problem or solution until you find the answer or understand what has happened

look for: to try to find something

Locate the phrasal verbs in the reading on page 126. Notice how they are used.

Focused Practice

A. *Read the sentences. Match each situation or cause with its correct effect.*

___f___ **1.** Our body and environment become too clean.

_____ **2.** The immune system doesn't come in contact with enough germs.

_____ **3.** Doctors in Israel prescribed fewer antibiotics in the summer months.

_____ **4.** Doctors prescribed antibiotics for many illnesses.

_____ **5.** The immune system attacks itself.

_____ **6.** Children grew up with siblings and pets.

a. They had fewer allergies.

b. Patients developed fewer ear infections.

c. People can get immune-related diseases such as allergies.

d. Some illnesses became resistant to antibiotic treatment.

e. The immune system weakens, and we get sick more easily.

_f._ We cannot fight off common germs.

B. *Read the statements below. Circle the opinion you agree with. Support your opinion by giving an example from your own experience or the experience of others.*

1. People should live in places that are (**more / less**) clean.

Example: _____

_____

2. People who live with dogs or cats have (**more / fewer**) allergies.

Example: _____

_____

3. Children with more siblings get sick (**more / less**) often.

Example: _____

_____

4. Doctors should prescribe antibiotics (**more / less**) often.

Example: _____

_____

5. Hand sanitizers are (**more / less**) helpful for children than adults.

Example: _____

_____

C. *Read the* Tip for Writers *and the examples. Then look at the highlighted pronouns below. Circle the word(s) the pronoun refers to.*

Examples:

==Immunologists== study the effect of germs on our bodies. ==They== have determined that even though some germs do make us sick, not all germs are bad.

==Midvedt== is a scientist . . . who studies good and bad germs. ==He== believes the simplest solution is to expose yourself to more germs.

noun   pronoun

Tip for Writers

Writers often use **pronouns** to refer back to a previous person, place, thing, or idea. Pronouns are words that stand for nouns, for example, *I, me, you, he, him, she, her, it, we, us, they,* and *them*. Using pronouns will help you vary your sentences and smooth out transitions between sentences and paragraphs in your essays.

1. This is the basis for the (hygiene hypothesis). It states that we cannot fight off common germs when the body and environment are *too* clean.

2. The immune system, which controls how the body fights diseases, cannot develop properly without germs. If we are not exposed to enough germs, it ends up losing strength.

3. When scientists developed antibiotics in the 1940s, doctors prescribed them for many illnesses.

4. When people got sick from these new bacteria, the antibiotics could not kill them anymore.

5. Because the bacteria were so powerful, doctors called them *superbugs*.

6. The scientists looked at 14,000 adults in New Zealand, Australia, the United States, and Europe. They found that children in larger families were healthier.

7. More scientists agree that a healthy immune system needs the right balance of good and bad germs. But they are still trying to figure out what the correct balance is and how to control it.

D. *Compare the health habits you learned about in "The Hygiene Hypothesis" to your own habits. Write a paragraph that explains your views about cleanliness and health. Try to use phrasal verbs and pronouns in your paragraph. Ask yourself these questions:*

- How do you try to solve common health problems, such as sore throats, the common cold, and ear infections?

- Do you believe in taking antibiotics, washing with antibacterial soaps and wipes, and using hand sanitizers? Why or why not?

_____

_____

_____

_____

_____

_____

_____

Writing a Problem-Solution Essay

In this unit, you are going to write a problem-solution essay about a health condition, a bad habit, or an environmental hazard. Problem-solution essays describe a problematic situation and ways to solve it. They may explain causes and/or effects of a problem. In addition, they usually emphasize the writer's opinion or advice about which solutions to the problem are the best.

Like all essays, a problem–solution essay contains three parts.

The Problem-Solution Essay

▶ Introduction
▶ Body
▶ Conclusion

Step 1   Prewriting

For a problem-solution essay, the first prewriting step is to select a topic that you know well enough to describe clearly. Select a problem that you feel strongly about and one that can be solved in specific ways. The prewriting step also includes brainstorming about the problem. *Why is it a problem? What are its causes and effects?* For example, if your topic is smoking among young people, you might ask yourself: *Why is smoking bad for teens? Why do they do it? What effects does it have on their health? What are the best, most effective ways to prevent or stop teens from smoking?*

Your Own Writing

Choosing Your Assignment

A. *Choose Assignment 1 or Assignment 2.*

  1. Describe a health-related problem that you or someone close to you has experienced. Choose a problem that you believe can be solved or improved. For example, you could write about a friend who suffers from bad migraine headaches or asthma, or an uncle who is overweight. Discuss the causes and effects of the problem and give two concrete solutions or ways to improve it.

  2. Describe a health problem that is caused by something natural or human-made in the environment. For example, you could discuss the hazards associated with second-hand cigarette smoke, or you could describe damage to the skin and eyes that can be caused by the rays of the sun. Give two concrete solutions or ways to improve the problem.

Finding Out More

A. *Learn more about your assignment before freewriting about it. Online or at the library, locate information about the health problem.*

  • Search for or look up the name of the health condition, bad habit, or environmental hazard.

  • Note the meanings of special words used to discuss the problem.

  • Locate new as well as older solutions to the problem.

B. *Freewrite for 10 minutes about your assignment. Here are some questions to get you started:*

- What are some of the causes and effects of the problem?

- How have people tried to solve or improve the problem?

- Which solutions have been the most helpful? the least helpful?

C. **Checking in.** *Work with a partner who chose the same assignment. Discuss the ideas and details you just wrote. Did your partner . . .*

- explain the causes and effects of the problem?

- describe why this is an important problem?

- suggest ways to solve or improve the problem?

Share your opinions about your partner's problem and solutions. Based on your discussion, make changes and additions to your writing.

D. *Complete the problem-solution chart. List your problem, explain why it's a problem (including its causes and effects), and suggest two ways to solve or improve it. Fill in as much information as you can. You will have a chance to review, change, or add information later in the unit.*

Problem (and Why it Is One)	Possible Solutions

■ THE INTRODUCTION

In a problem-solution essay, the introduction usually gives background information about the problem, for example, why it happens, who it affects, and when or where it occurs. It may also describe how people feel about the problem and/or define key words people use to discuss it.

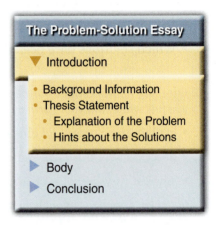

Example:

Background Information:

Doing exercise is important to stay healthy, but fewer and fewer people are able to exercise regularly. This is especially true for adults. Adults often complain that they don't have enough time to follow a daily fitness, or exercise, routine because of their many work, school, or family responsibilities. On the other hand, doctors tell us that regular exercise is essential to keeping our bodies healthy and working properly. Not getting enough exercise can lead to poor health, but there are some simple steps people can take to increase their physical activity.

The thesis statement briefly describes the topic and gives the controlling idea. The controlling idea explains why something is a problem and hints at the possible solutions you will present in the body of your essay. The thesis statement may be one sentence or two sentences.

Example:

topic	why it's a problem	hints at solutions

Not getting enough exercise can lead to poor health, but there are some simple steps people can take to increase their physical activity.

Focused Practice

A. *Read the following essay assignment. Then decide which of the details you might use as background information for an introductory paragraph on this topic. Check (✓) the sentences you choose. Discuss your answers with a partner.*

> ***Describe a health problem that is caused by too much exposure to the sun. Give two solutions or ways to improve this problem.***

_____ **1.** Every time people go outside, they are exposed to the sun.

_____ **2.** *Sun exposure* means not being protected from the sun's rays.

_____ **3.** Many young people spend a lot of time on the beach sunbathing because they want a deep, rich tan.

_____ **4.** A little sun can benefit the skin, but too much exposure can lead to skin damage and even skin cancer.

_____ **5.** Sunburns feel better when you put aloe lotions or vitamin E on them.

_____ **6.** Some skin cancers can be treated fairly easily, but others are extremely dangerous and hard to stop.

_____ **7.** Because serious effects don't appear until much later in life, people often ignore the health warnings about sun exposure.

_____ **8.** Experts say that overexposure to the sun is a real problem.

B. *Review the background information you chose in Exercise A. Then check (✓) the sentence(s) that would be the best thesis statement for the essay. Discuss your answers with a partner.*

_____ **1.** Even though the sun can cause serious burns, many people ignore this fact and get skin damage as a result.

_____ **2.** Skin damage is a big problem and can have very bad effects. Prevention is the best policy.

_____ **3.** Sun exposure can seriously affect people's health; however, people can avoid the health hazards of too much sun in several ways.

C. *Look at the model of an introductory paragraph for an essay on the topic in Exercise A. Discuss the questions with a partner.*

> Every time people go outside, they are exposed to the sun. *Sun exposure* means not being protected from the sun's rays. A little sun can benefit the skin, but too much exposure can lead to skin damage and even skin cancer. Because serious effects don't appear until much later in life, people often ignore the health warnings about sun exposure. Yet, experts say that overexposure to the sun is a real problem. Sun exposure can seriously affect people's health; however, people can deal with the health hazards of too much sun in several ways.

1. What is the problem?

2. When does the problem occur? Why does it occur?

3. What does *sun exposure* mean?

4. Why do some people ignore the problem of overexposure to the sun?

5. What is the thesis statement? Underline it.

6. Do you think the thesis is effective? Why or why not?

Your Own Writing

Finding Out More

A. *Do more research about the health problem you chose for your essay.*

- Online or at the library, locate other supporting details connected to your topic.

- Keep the following questions in mind: *Who does the problem affect? When and where does the problem occur? What are the most important causes and effects of the problem? How can the problem best be solved?*

B. *Take notes on what you found out. Record important facts or quotations about the health problem. Add new information to the problem-solution chart on page 131. Use this information when you write your essay. Be sure to note key information on your sources. (See the Appendix on pages 150–151.)*

C. Checking in. *Share your information with a partner. Did your partner . . .*

- gather enough background information about the health problem?

- find at least two good solutions or ways to improve the problem?

- use at least three reliable sources?

Planning Your Introduction

A. *List the background information you will need to include in your introduction.*

_____

_____

B. *Write a draft of your thesis statement. Make sure your thesis statement clearly explains the problem and hints at the solutions you will present and justify in the body of your essay. Look back at your freewriting and problem-solution chart to help you.*

_____

_____

C. Checking in. *Share your thesis statement with a partner. Did your partner . . .*

- clearly explain the health problem in the thesis statement?

- focus on an illness, a bad habit, or an environmentally caused health problem?

- let you know that solutions will be presented in the body of the essay?

Tell your partner what you like about his or her thesis statement. If you have any suggestions for improving it, share them. Based on your partner's feedback, you may want to rewrite your thesis statement.

■ THE BODY

In a problem-solution essay, you begin by convincing your reader that a problem exists and is serious. You then give one or more solutions to the problem. There are many ways to structure a problem-solution essay. One of the simplest ways is to present the problem in detail in the first body paragraph and give the solutions in the second body paragraph.

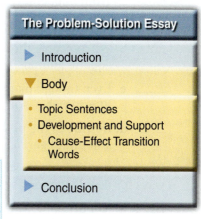

Your essay will use the following pattern:

Paragraph 1	Introduction to the Problem + Thesis Statement
Paragraph 2	Problem: Reasons Why It's Serious
Paragraph 3	Solutions: Steps to Take and How to Follow Them
Paragraph 4	Conclusion

Writing Topic Sentences

As you learned in the previous two units, each body paragraph must have a clearly stated controlling idea. In a problem-solution essay, the topic sentences introduce the writer's focus on reasons for the problems and ways to solve or prevent them. In a four-paragraph essay, writers often indicate their transition from problems to solutions in the second body paragraph. Here is an example of a thesis statement and two topic sentences for a problem-solution essay. Notice how the three sentences are connected to each other.

Example:

Thesis Statement: Not getting enough exercise can lead to poor health, but there are some simple steps people can take to increase their activity.

Topic Sentence 1: There are two major reasons why not exercising causes problems for people.

transition from problems to solutions
Topic Sentence 2: To increase their activity levels, adults can find both practical and creative solutions.

Focused Practice

Read each thesis statement. Then check (✓) the two sentences that would be the best topic sentences for an essay on this topic. Discuss your answers with a partner.

  1. Sun exposure can seriously affect people's health; however, people can deal with the health hazards of too much sun in several ways.

_____ **a.** Bad sunburns can make people develop more wrinkles when they get older.

_____ **b.** Too much exposure to the sun has a bad effect on our body for a number of reasons.

_____ **c.** Despite these problems, there are ways for people to protect their skin from the sun and repair damage.

_____ **d.** Most people know about the health hazards of too much sun, but they don't do anything to protect themselves.

(continued)

2. Littering damages the environment, but people can take steps to prevent this situation from happening.

_____ **a.** Littering has negative effects on the environment for various reasons.

_____ **b.** When people throw trash into rivers, they can pollute the water and hurt aquatic animals.

_____ **c.** Even though many people know about the problems associated with littering, they still do it.

_____ **d.** In spite of the problems, there are two specific ways people can reduce the amount of garbage they produce.

3. Drinking too little water stops the body from working properly, yet there are easy ways for people to increase the amount of water they take in.

_____ **a.** Not drinking water regularly can make people become dehydrated.

_____ **b.** To change this habit, people need to look for simple ways to increase the amount of water they take in.

_____ **c.** Not drinking enough water is a bad habit for several reasons.

_____ **d.** Although many drinks contain water, such as soft drinks, tea, and coffee, pure water is always the best choice.

4. Those college students who suffer from lack of sleep can take simple steps to increase the amount of sleep they get each night.

_____ **a.** Not getting enough sleep is problematic for college students for two reasons.

_____ **b.** Some students say that, with hours of homework to do each night, they are too busy to get enough sleep.

_____ **c.** To minimize these problems, college students can change their habits in two important ways.

_____ **d.** Many college students think that drinking lots of caffeine will keep them alert and awake, but these are only temporary fixes.

Developing a Body Paragraph about a Problem

As you learned in the previous units, writers support their body paragraphs with various kinds of evidence, including reasons, facts, examples, and explanations. For a paragraph about a problem, writers can include specific reasons why their problem is serious using listing-order transition signals like *first (of all)*, *for one*, *second (of all)*, *in addition*, and *finally* to introduce each reason. They may support their reasons by explaining the causes or effects of the problem. To end the body paragraph, some writers add a sentence that summarizes the reasons for the problem; this is optional.

Example:

There are two major reasons why not exercising causes problems for people. First of all, it can make our muscles weaker. When people don't exercise, their muscles lose strength and become tense. Consequently, people can get hurt more easily when they have to lift heavy objects or run quickly. Due to inactivity, people are also more likely to pull and strain muscles when they stretch their bodies too far. In addition, a lack of physical activity is bad for the heart. The heart is also a muscle. As a result, it needs to be exercised too. People who do not increase their heart rate regularly with moderate exercise like jogging or swimming have weaker hearts. Because of this, they can be at a greater risk for heart problems, such as heart disease and heart attacks, when they get older. If people do not exercise at all, all of their muscles, including the heart, will suffer.

When writers discuss a problem, they may use cause–effect transition words, including the ones in the chart, to show how one action or situation affects another.

Causes	Effects
as a result of because of due to	as a result consequently therefore thus

Examples:

Because of this, they can be at a greater risk of heart problems when they get older, such as heart disease and heart attacks.

Due to inactivity, people are also more likely to pull and strain muscles when they stretch their bodies too far.

When people don't exercise, their muscles lose strength and become tense. Consequently, people can get hurt more easily when they have to lift heavy objects or run quickly.

The heart is also a muscle. As a result, it needs to be exercised too.

Focused Practice

A. On page 133, you read an introductory paragraph for a problem-solution essay about overexposure to the sun. Now read the writer's thesis statement again and the first body paragraph. Then discuss the questions with a partner.

> **Thesis Statement:** Sun exposure can seriously affect people's health; however, people can deal with the health hazards of too much sun in several ways.
>
> Too much exposure to the sun has a bad effect on our body for a number of reasons. For one, people, especially those who are fair skinned, can get sunburns. Skin is sensitive to sunlight. Because of this, it can turn pink or red when it is not protected. Bad sunburns can be uncomfortable, painful, and damaging to the skin. Furthermore, as a result of overexposure, health problems can crop up later in life. When skin is damaged over many years, it cannot repair itself. Consequently, people who have had many sunburns can develop more wrinkles when they get older. They also experience premature aging, where wrinkles show up sooner than normal. In addition, studies have shown that people who sunbathe end up being at a much higher risk for skin cancer. Due to the sun, people suffer from mild and serious health problems.

1. Where are reasons for the problem introduced? Underline the topic sentence.
2. Why is overexposure to the sun a problem? Check (✔) three main reasons.
3. Which transition words introduce each specific reason? Circle them.
4. Which transition words signal causes? Underline them.
5. Which transition words signal effects? Double underline them.
6. Circle the sentence that sums up all of the information in the paragraph.

B. Rewrite the sentences. Change the highlighted part of the sentence using the transition words in parentheses. Use correct punctuation. The first one is done for you.

1. Because there are antibiotics, people can fight off bacteria more easily.

   As a result of antibiotics, people can fight off bacteria more easily. (**as a result of**)

2. Tore Midvedt believes in the hygiene hypothesis, so he suggests being less dirty.

   _____ (**therefore**)

3. Students can easily lose their concentration because they sleep too little.

   _____ (**because of**)

4. Not drinking water dehydrates you, so you might get headaches or feel sick.

   _____ (**consequently**)

Developing a Body Paragraph about Solutions

In a problem-solution essay, the second body paragraph can offer solutions to the problem. As in the first body paragraph, writers often use listing-order transition words to introduce their specific solutions or suggestions. The supporting sentences may give steps on how to follow the solutions or provide reasons why the solutions are useful or important to follow. Writers often finish the paragraph with a sentence that summarizes the solutions. Once again, it is optional, but it can tie the parts of an essay together.

Example:

   To increase their activity levels, adults can find both practical and creative solutions. First of all, they can make choices throughout the day to exercise the body more. For instance, instead of riding the elevator or escalator, people can take the stairs to get their muscles working and heart pumping. If people live close to a supermarket, they can choose to walk instead of driving just a couple of miles. Second of all, people can stick to a short but regular exercise routine. When adults finish work, they can devote a half hour to exercising before doing housework or relaxing on the couch. For example, they might take a short walk around the neighborhood or stop by a local gym to work out before going home. There are many easy ways for people to exercise more; it just takes a little planning and creativity.

Focused Practice

A. *Work with a partner. Read the body paragraph about solutions. Then fill in the two sentences that best introduce each solution.*

   Despite these problems, there are ways for people to protect their skin from the sun and repair damage. First of all, _____

_____.

Sunscreen contains special chemicals that prevent burning. Using sunscreen is necessary when people are exposed to the sun for long periods of time, such as when sunbathing, taking a walk outside, or working in the garden. Second of all,

_____

_____.

The simplest solution is to eat healthy foods such as fruits and vegetables. They have vitamins that the body uses to repair skin and make it strong again. In addition, using lotions with vitamin A can promote healing of sunburned skin.

---

   a. people should use sunscreens that contain vitamin A

   b. people can take different steps to prevent sun damage

   c. people need to use sunscreen to keep their skin healthy

   d. when people do have sun-damaged skin, they can also take steps to fix it

B. *Look again at the body paragraph in Exercise A on page 139. Write a concluding sentence for the paragraph. Discuss your sentence with a partner.*

_____

_____

Your Own Writing

Planning Your Body Paragraphs

A. *Before you begin writing your body paragraphs, complete the following outline. Copy your thesis statement from page 134.*

Problem-Solution Essay

Thesis Statement: _____

▶ Body Paragraph 1

  ▶ Topic Sentence: _____

    ▶ Supporting Details

      • _____

      • _____

      • _____

  ▶ Summary Sentence (Optional): _____

  _____

▶ Body Paragraph 2

  ▶ Topic Sentence: _____

    ▶ Supporting Details

      • _____

      • _____

      • _____

  ▶ Summary Sentence (Optional): _____

  _____

B. Checking in. *Share your outline with a partner. Tell your partner which . . .*

• details about the problem might need more explanation.

• solution seems most convincing to you and why.

Based on your partner's feedback, you may want to rewrite parts of your outline.

■ THE CONCLUSION

As with the essays you wrote in Units 4 and 5, you will return to the thesis statement in your conclusion and express your final thoughts and recommendations.

Here are two strategies you might want to use to end your problem-solution essay about a specific health condition, bad habit, or environmental hazard.

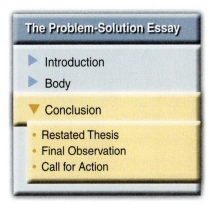

1. Add a final observation about how people view the problem.

2. Make a "call for action" that asks people to do something to help solve the problem.

Example:

In order to increase physical activity, adults should find practical and creative ways to exercise more regularly. Although many adults complain that they are too busy to exercise, they need to realize the enormous benefits that come from doing just a little bit each day. Adults should figure out a simple way to add regular exercise to their daily routine by reviewing and rearranging some of their day-to-day activities. The earlier they start, the sooner they will start feeling the benefits.

restated thesis   observation   call for action

Focused Practice

Read the model of a concluding paragraph. Discuss the questions with a partner.

> In all, there are several ways people can prevent and minimize the problems brought about by overexposure to the sun. Most people understand the dangerous link between sun exposure and sunburns, wrinkles, and cancer, but they still put themselves at risk by not protecting themselves or repairing damaged skin. People need to take the dangers of sun exposure more seriously. They should put on sunscreen whenever they are outside for a long time, and they should consume fruits and vegetables in order to help their skin stay healthy in the sun.

1. What is the writer's restated thesis? Circle the sentence.

2. According to the writer, how do people view the problem? Underline the sentence that gives the writer's observation.

3. What is the writer's call for action? Double underline the sentence(s).

Your Own Writing

Planning Your Conclusion

A. *How will you rephrase your thesis statement in the conclusion? List your ideas here.*

_____

_____

B. *What strategy will you use to close the essay?*

_____

_____

C. Checking in. *Share your ideas with a partner. Did your partner . . .*

- choose an effective strategy?

- discover a new and interesting way to phrase his or her thesis statement?

Writing Your First Draft

Read the **Tip for Writers.** *Review your notes on pages 131, 134, and 140. Then write the first draft of your essay. When you are finished, give your essay a working title. Hand in your draft to your teacher.*

> **Tip for Writers**
>
> When you write your first draft, check that you have used pronouns correctly and effectively.

Step 3   Revising

Revising your work is an essential part of the writing process. This is your opportunity to be sure that your essay has all the important pieces and that it is clear.

Focused Practice

A. *You have read parts of this problem-solution essay already. Now read it from beginning to end, and notice how the parts fit together.*

> ### Here Comes the Sun
>
> Every time people go outside, they are exposed to the sun. *Sun exposure* means not being protected from the sun's rays. A little sun can benefit the skin, but too much exposure can lead to skin damage and even skin cancer. Because serious effects don't appear until much later in life, people often ignore the health warnings about sun exposure. Yet, experts say that overexposure to the sun is a
>
> *(continued)*

real problem. Sun exposure can seriously affect people's health; however, people can deal with the health hazards of too much sun in several ways.

Too much exposure to the sun has a bad effect on our body for a number of reasons. For one, people, especially those who are fair skinned, can get sunburns. Skin is sensitive to sunlight. Because of this, it can turn pink or red when it is not protected. Bad sunburns can be uncomfortable, painful, and damaging to the skin. Furthermore, as a result of overexposure, health problems can crop up later in life. When skin is damaged over many years, it cannot repair itself. Consequently, people who have had many sunburns can develop more wrinkles when they get older. They also experience premature aging, where wrinkles show up sooner than normal. In addition, studies have shown that people who sunbathe end up being at a much higher risk of skin cancer. Due to the sun, people suffer from mild and serious health problems.

Despite these problems, there are ways for people to protect their skin from the sun and repair damage. First of all, people need to use sunscreen to keep their skin healthy. Sunscreen contains special chemicals that prevent burning. Using sunscreen is necessary when people are exposed to the sun for long periods of time, such as when sunbathing, taking a walk outside, or working in the garden. Second of all, when people do have sun-damaged skin, they can also take steps to fix it. The simplest solution is to eat healthy foods such as fruits and vegetables. They have vitamins that the body uses to repair skin and make it strong again. In addition, using lotions with vitamin A can promote healing of sunburned skin. With sunscreen, a good diet, and lotions, people can keep their skin healthy in the sun.

In all, there are several ways people can prevent and minimize the problems brought about overexposure to the sun. Most people understand the dangerous link between sun exposure and sunburns, wrinkles, and cancer, but they still put themselves at risk by not protecting themselves or repairing damaged skin. People need to take the dangers of sun exposure more seriously. They should put on sunscreen whenever they are outside for a long time, and they should consume fruits and vegetables in order to help their skin stay healthy in the sun.

B. *Work with a partner. Answer the questions about the essay.*

1. What kinds of background information appear in the introduction? Check (✔) the sentences that provide background information.

2. Underline the thesis statement, the topic sentences for the body paragraphs, and the restated thesis in the conclusion. How are the sentences related?

(continued)

3. What transition words connect the parts of the essay? Circle them.

4. What causes and effects in paragraph 2 support and develop the problem? Check (✓) three kinds of support and development in the paragraph.

5. What specific steps and examples in paragraph 3 support and develop solutions for the problem? Check (✓) three kinds of support and development in the paragraph.

6. What kind(s) of concluding strategies does the writer use to finish the essay? Are they effective? Why or why not?

_____

_____

_____

C. Checking in. *Discuss your marked-up essays with another pair of students. Then in your group, share one thing about the essay that you found the most interesting. Explain your answer.*

Building Word Knowledge

The writer included some phrasal verbs in "Here Comes the Sun," including *end up* and *brought about*.

Look at the sentences from the essay. Choose the correct definition for the highlighted phrasal verbs.

1. A little sun can benefit the skin, but too much exposure can lead to skin damage and even skin cancer.

    a. cause

    b. happen

    c. finish

2. People can deal with the health hazards of too much sun in several ways.

    a. share

    b. understand

    c. handle

3. As a result of overexposure, health problems can crop up later in life.

    a. grow

    b. happen

    c. worsen

4. They also experience premature aging, where wrinkles <mark>show up</mark> sooner than normal.

    a. appear

    b. stop

    c. take

5. They should <mark>put on</mark> sunscreen whenever they are outside for a long time.

    a. apply

    b. buy

    c. take

Your Own Writing

Revising Your Draft

A. *Reread the first draft of your essay. Use the Revision Checklist to identify parts of your writing that might need improvement.*

B. *Review your plans and notes and your responses to the Revision Checklist. Then revise your first draft. Save your revised essay. You will look at it again in the next section.*

Revision Checklist

Did you . . .

☐ give enough background information in your introduction?

☐ express your controlling idea in the thesis statement?

☐ present the problem clearly in your first body paragraph?

☐ give two convincing solutions to the problem in your second body paragraph?

☐ use a variety of transition words to connect your sentences and paragraphs?

☐ use pronouns to make your writing flow more smoothly?

☐ restate the controlling idea of your essay in your conclusion?

☐ use an effective concluding strategy?

☐ use phrasal verbs correctly?

☐ give your essay a good title?

GRAMMAR PRESENTATION

Before you hand in your revised essay, you must check it for any errors in grammar, punctuation, and spelling. In this section, you will learn about gerunds. You will focus on this grammar when you edit and proofread your essay.

Gerunds: Subject and Object

Grammar Notes	Examples
1. A **gerund** (**base form of verb + -ing**) is a verb that we use **like a noun**. **BE CAREFUL!** There are often **spelling changes** when you add -ing. Form the **negative** by placing *not* before the gerund.	• **Doing** exercise is important to stay healthy. • **Taking** antibiotics may lead to more infections. • **Getting** sick is a natural part of everyone's life. BASE FORM GERUND take tak**ing** get get**ting** • **Not taking** antibiotics may result in fewer ear infections. • **Not getting** enough exercise can lead to poor health.

2. A gerund can be the **subject** of a sentence. It is always <u>singular</u>. Use the third-person-singular form of the verb after gerunds.
 	
 BE CAREFUL! Do not confuse a <u>gerund</u> with the <u>progressive form</u> of a verb.
	• **Littering** *damages* the environment.
	 • **Washing** your hands *helps* to prevent exposure to germs.
	
	     gerund
	 • **Exercising** makes your muscles stronger.
	
	     progressive form
	 • He **is exercising** right now.

3. A gerund can also be the **object** of certain verbs. Use a gerund **after these verbs**: advise dislike prevent stop avoid finish quit suggest consider keep recommend understand	• The doctor *advised* **exercising** more. • She *avoids* **eating** unhealthy foods. • I *dislike* **taking** a lot of medication. • They *keep* **covering** their mouths. • That will *prevent* **infecting** others. • He *recommends* **being** less clean.
4. A gerund can also be the **object of a preposition**. Use a gerund **after prepositions** such as: about before in to against by of with at for on without Because **gerunds** are nouns, they can be the object of a preposition. **REMEMBER:** Form the **negative** by placing *not* before the gerund.	• People can protect their skin *by using* sunscreen. • Stretch *before* **exercising**. • I am *against* **overusing** antibiotics. • Living with pets prevented the immune system *from* **attacking** itself. • They are relieved **about** *not* **having** allergies anymore.

Focused Practice

A. *Read the paragraph. Underline the gerunds. There are ten. The first one is already underlined. Find and underline nine more.*

Not <u>getting</u> enough sleep can cause students many problems. First of all, lack of sleep can prevent students from being able to concentrate in class. Not concentrating can have other consequences, such as missing important information from the teacher, feeling lost in class, and doing poorly on exams and homework. In addition, sleeping too little also affects how students perform outside of class. When they are studying, they often have trouble with staying focused on their work. Furthermore, they often cannot avoid falling asleep even though they haven't finished doing all of their homework assignments.

B. *Complete the sentences with gerunds. Use the verbs from the box. Choose between affirmative and negative.*

become	find	grow	prescribe
fight	get	help	wash

1. The researchers are working on _____ the right balance of good and bad germs.

2. Doctors recommend _____ your hands before and after every meal.

3. _____ enough germs is the main idea of the hygiene hypothesis.

4. Some germs make us sick, but others are capable of _____ our bodies.

5. _____ up with pets may reduce allergies in adulthood.

6. A healthy immune system is better at _____ off germs.

7. Today, doctors prefer _____ antibiotics only when it is absolutely necessary.

8. Taking fewer antibiotics may prevent the body from _____ resistant to superbugs.

C. *Read and edit the paragraph. There are nine errors in the use or spelling of gerunds. The first error has been corrected for you. Find and correct eight more.*

Scientists have not found a cure for the common cold, but some researchers
have shown that people can reduce symptoms without ~~take~~ *taking* medicine. In fact, use
natural methods sometimes works better for certain people. One study suggests
that eat chicken soup helps. Having chicken soup reduces nasal congestion, which
means that viruses cannot stay in the nose as long. Drink hot tea with lemon may
also be beneficial. Like chicken soup, hot tea helps the nose from becomeing
too congested and stops it from runing. Add lemon will also give the body extra
vitamin C and make the immune system better at fight a cold. When a cold is
accompanied by a cough, researchers have found that honey can also help. When
young children took honey at bedtime, they coughed less at night. For people who
prefer don't taking medicine for the common cold, one of these natural remedies
just might be the solution.

D. *Write five sentences related to the topic you chose on page 130.* Use *gerunds as subjects* or *objects.* *These may be sentences you already have in your essay.*

1. _____

_____

2. _____

_____

3. _____

_____

4. _____

_____

5. _____

_____

Your Own Writing

Editing Your Draft

A. *Use the Editing Checklist to edit and proofread your essay.*

B. *Prepare a clean copy of the final draft of your essay and hand it in to your teacher.*

Editing Checklist
Did you . . .
☐ include gerunds as subjects and objects and use them correctly?
☐ use correct verb forms, punctuation, and spelling?
☐ use phrasal verbs correctly?
☐ use pronouns and other words correctly?

Appendix

■ RESEARCHING A TOPIC

Use the library and the Internet to find out more about your topic. For each source you use, record the author, title, date, publisher, and medium (e.g., print, Web, DVD).

Using Resources. The library contains a wide range of printed books, magazines, and reference materials (encyclopedias, atlases, and books of facts) that you can use to find information. Look for two or three books or articles with information about your topic. Although you can begin researching your topic in an encyclopedia, most instructors will not allow you to use this information as a cited source in your paragraph or essay. If you find information in an encyclopedia, look at the end of the entry for titles of individual books and articles about your topic; try to locate and use these sources.

One of the quickest ways to search for information is to use the Internet. Today, many books, articles, and reference books are available online. To do an online search, select keywords or a key question. Then type it into a search engine, such as Google, Yahoo, or Bing. Keep your online search as narrow as possible. Otherwise you will have to look through too many sources.

Suppose that you wanted to find out about the legally blind musher Rachael Scdoris who competed in the Iditarod in 2005. Here are some examples of specific keywords and questions that would help you find sources about her.

Examples:

Keywords:

Iditarod competitor Rachael Scdoris
Rachael Scdoris and the 2005 Iditarod

Key Questions:

Who is the Iditarod competitor Rachael Scdoris?
What happened when Rachael Scdoris competed in the 2005 Iditarod?

Evaluating Resources. Once you locate a source, think critically about it.

- When was it published? Is it up to date?
- Is it published by a well-known and reliable place (e.g., a mainstream newspaper or government website)?
- Does it present a balanced and unbiased point of view, or is it only expressing one person's opinion?
- Does it contain facts that can be double-checked in another source?

Evaluate each source you use, especially, the sources you find on the Internet. Some Internet sites contain inaccurate information, so limit your sources to trusted sites.

■ CITING SOURCES IN YOUR WRITING

When you are writing a paragraph or essay, always acknowledge your sources of information or any wording that is not your own. If you do not cite your sources, including the words, ideas, or research that you have borrowed from others, you are *plagiarizing*, or stealing other people's ideas. This is a serious offense that is treated very severely in an academic environment.

In colleges and universities, one of the most commonly used styles for handling citations is the MLA (Modern Language Association) style. According to the MLA style, you cite your sources in two places: within the text and in a "Works Cited" list.*

In-Text Citations. Most of the wording in your paragraphs and essays should be your own. When you paraphrase or quote what other people have said or researched, give a brief citation for the source in parentheses at the end of the sentence. If you have already mentioned the author within the sentence, you do not need to repeat the name at the end.

Examples:

Citing a Fact: According to a 2011 report, Twitter has only 21 million active users (Bennett).

Citing a Paraphrase: The legendary journalist spoke of the need to support public broadcasting (Moyers). [or] Bill Moyers, a legendary journalist, spoke of the need to support public broadcasting.

Citing a Quote: On her website, the legally blind musher says: "I hope my story can help encourage others to pursue their dreams" (Scdoris).

A List of Works Cited. At the end of your writing, provide a list of all the sources you have cited. Type "Works Cited" at the top of the list and center the heading. Then organize your sources alphabetically according to the author's last name. If the source has no author, alphabetize it according to its title. Indent the second line of the source.

The basic format for individual citations and a "Works Cited" list is shown in the examples below.

Examples:

For Articles: Author. "Article Title." *Magazine Title* date: page no. medium.

For Books: Author. *Book Title.* publisher, date: page no. medium.

For Personal Interviews: Name of Interviewee. Personal interview. date.

For Websites: Website title. publisher, date. medium. date accessed. <URL>

Works Cited

Collum, Danny Duncan. "How to save journalism: can a government-subsidized press save democracy?" *Sojourners* June 2009: 40. Print.

Miller, Claire Cain. "The New News Junkie Is Online and On the Phone." *New York Times* 1 Mar. 2010. Print.

Noone, Joan. Personal interview. 20 July 2011.

---

* The format for citing other sources can also be found in MLA handbooks, on the websites for most college and university libraries in North America, or by searching the Internet using the keywords *MLA style*. For electronic sources, MLA style no longer requires writers to include web addresses, or URLs, but some instructors may still require them. Some instructors will also allow you to use citation generators that are available online. Check with your teacher about his or her requirements.

Index

Acknowledgments

Focus on Writing 3 was a true collaboration. Many thanks go to the editorial team at Pearson who saw this project from beginning to end. I'd especially like to thank Editorial Manager Debbie Sistino for the opportunity to be a part of this project, and Joan Poole, my senior development editor, who was with me every step of the way and whose expertise was vital to the success of this book. Thanks also to Series Editor John Beaumont for his inspiration and support.

I am grateful to everyone who had a hand in the design, development, and production of *Focus on Writing 3*: Senior Production Editors Danielle Belfiore and Jaime Lieber; Production Editor Adina Zoltan; Development Editor Nan Clarke; Copy Editor Elizabeth Verzariu; and Proofreader Leigh Stolle. You were all an awesome team!

I would also like to thank my colleagues who make teaching at Lone Star College– North Harris a true pleasure, including Dr. Head and Dr. Harrison, and my fellow ESOL professors, David, Pat, Gwen, Katie, Janet, Alice, and Erin. Thanks also to my wonderful students, who are always an inspiration and make me look forward to teaching each and every day.

Finally, to Stefanie, Tamsin, and Erin, you mean the world to me and always keep me grounded. Thanks for your patience, humor, and for just being you.

Colin Ward

Credits